THE INFINITE TENDERNESS OF GOD

MEDITATIONS ON THE GOSPELS

POPE FRANCIS

THE INFINITE TENDERNESS OF GOD

MEDITATIONS ON THE GOSPELS

POPE FRANCIS

Compiled by Jeanne Kun

Copyright © 2016 Libreria Editrice Vaticana
Compilation Copyright © 2016 The Word Among Us Press

Published by The Word Among Us Press
7115 Guilford Road
Frederick, Maryland 21704
www.wau.org

20 19 18 17 16   1 2 3 4 5

ISBN: 978-1-59325-287-8
eISBN: 978-1-59325-479-7

Pope Francis' homilies and addresses taken from the Vatican translation
and can be found on the Vatican website, www.vatican.va.
Used with permission of Libreria Editrice Vaticana.

Scripture texts used in this work are taken from the Catholic Edition of
Revised Standard Version Bible, copyright © 1965, 1966 by the Division of
Christian Education of the National Council of the Churches of Christ in
the United States of America. Used with permission. All rights reserved.

Cover design by Andrea Alvarez
Cover photo: Getty Images
Inside text photo: Thinkstock

Made and printed in the United States of America

Library of Congress Control Number: 2015957292

CONTENTS

INTRODUCTION

"Who is Jesus for you? Are you with Jesus? Do you try to comprehend him in his word? Do you read the Gospel, each day a passage from the Gospel, to learn to know Jesus? Do you carry a small Gospel in your pocket, handbag, to read it, in whatever place? Because the more we are with him, the more the desire to be with him grows."

—POPE FRANCIS, ANGELUS ADDRESS, AUGUST 23, 2015

Pope Francis is convinced that if we really want to become a friend of Jesus, then we need to read the Gospels. That's why he encourages us to carry the Gospels with us—so that we can read a passage anytime or anywhere. And what better way to explore the Gospels than to explore them with the Holy Father!

As you might expect, these meditations are filled with Pope Francis' characteristic warmth, wisdom, and wit. His pastoral advice is based on his keen understanding of our human condition. The reflections reveal his own profound love for Jesus as well as his burning desire that all men and women would come to a deep encounter with Jesus.

The Word Among Us Press is delighted to bring you these reflections, which are taken from homilies, addresses, and speeches given by the Holy Father since the beginning of his pontificate. Many of these texts were delivered at St. Peter's Square, but others were proclaimed during the pope's extensive travels throughout the world.

We pray that as you meditate on the Gospels with Pope Francis, you will discover who Jesus is for you and grow both in your love for him and your desire to be with him.

Jeanne Kun

1. MARY, "MOTHER OF YES"
LUKE 1:26-38

In the Gospel, we have just heard the greeting of the angel to Mary: "*Rejoice, full of grace. The Lord is with you*" [cf. Luke 1:28]. Rejoice, Mary, rejoice. Upon hearing this greeting, Mary was confused and asked herself what it could mean. She did not fully understand what was happening. But she knew that the angel came from God, and so she said yes. Mary is the "Mother of Yes." Yes to God's dream, yes to God's care, yes to God's will.

It was a yes that, as we know, was not easy to live. A yes that bestowed no privileges or distinctions. Simeon told her in his prophecy, "A sword will pierce your heart" (cf. Luke 2:35), and indeed it did. That is why we love her so much. We find in her a true mother, one who helps us to keep faith and hope alive in the midst of complicated situations. Pondering Simeon's prophecy, we would do well to reflect briefly on three difficult moments in Mary's life.

1. The first moment: the birth of Jesus. There was no room for them. They had no house, no dwelling to receive her son. There was no place where she could give birth. They had no family close by; they were alone. The only place available was a stall of animals. Surely she remembered the words of the angel: "Rejoice, Mary, the Lord is with you." She might well have asked herself, "Where is he now?"

2. The second moment: the flight to Egypt. They had to leave, to go into exile. Not only was there no room for them, no family

nearby, but their lives were also in danger. They had to depart to a foreign land. They were persecuted migrants on account of the envy and greed of the king. There, too, she might well have asked, "What happened to all those things promised by the angel?"

3. The third moment: Jesus' death on the cross. There can be no more difficult experience for a mother than to witness the death of her child. It is heartrending. We see Mary there, at the foot of the cross, like every mother, strong, faithful, staying with her child even to his death, death on the cross. There, too, she might well have asked, "What happened to all those things promised to me by the angel?" Then we see her encouraging and supporting the disciples.

We contemplate her life, and we feel understood, we feel heard. We can sit down to pray with her and use a common language in the face of the countless situations we encounter each day. We can identify with many situations in her life. We can tell her what is happening in our lives because she understands.

Mary is the woman of faith; she is the Mother of the Church; she believed. Her life testifies that God does not deceive us, that God does not abandon his people, even in moments or situations when it might seem that he is not there. Mary was the first of her son's disciples, and in moments of difficulty she kept alive the hope of the apostles. With probably more than one key, they were locked in the upper room, due to fear. A woman attentive to the needs of others, she could say—when it seemed like the feast and joy were at an end—"See, they have no wine" (cf. John 2:3). She was the woman who went to stay with her cousin "about three months" (Luke 1:56), so that Elizabeth would not be alone as she prepared to give birth. That is our Mother, so good and so kind, she who accompanies us in our lives.

—HOMILY, MARIAN SHRINE OF CAACUPÉ, PARAGUAY, JULY 11, 2015

2. AN ENCOUNTER BRIDGING GENERATIONS
LUKE 1:39-45

Today we accept the Gospel we have just heard as a Gospel of encounter: the encounter between young and old, an encounter full of joy, full of faith, and full of hope.

Mary is young, very young. Elizabeth is elderly, yet God's mercy was manifested in her, and for six months now, with her husband Zechariah, she has been expecting a child.

Here too, Mary shows us the way: she set out to visit her elderly kinswoman, to stay with her, to help her, of course, but also and above all to learn from her—an elderly person—a wisdom of life.

Today's first reading echoes in various ways the fourth commandment: "Honor your father and your mother, so that your days may be long in the land that the Lord your God is giving you" (cf. Exodus 20:12). A people has no future without such an encounter between generations, without children being able to accept with gratitude the witness of life from the hands of their parents. And part of this gratitude for those who gave you life is also gratitude for our heavenly Father.

There are times when generations of young people, for complex historical and cultural reasons, feel a deeper need to be independent from their parents, "breaking free," as it were, from the legacy of the older generation. It is a kind of adolescent rebellion. But unless the encounter, the meeting of generations, is reestablished, unless a new and fruitful intergenerational equilibrium is restored, what results is a serious impoverishment for everyone, and the freedom which prevails in society is actually a false freedom, which almost always becomes a form of authoritarianism. . . .

And so we return to this "icon" full of joy and hope, full of faith and charity. We can imagine that the Virgin Mary, visiting the home of Elizabeth, would have heard her and her husband, Zechariah, praying in the words of today's responsorial psalm: "You, O Lord, are my hope, / my trust, O LORD, from my youth. / . . . Do not cast me off in the time of old age; / do not forsake me when my strength is spent. . . . So even to old age and gray hairs, / O God, do not forsake me, / till I proclaim your might / to all the generations to come" (cf. Psalm 71:5, 9, 18). The young Mary listened, and she kept all these things in her heart. The wisdom of Elizabeth and Zechariah enriched her young spirit. They were no experts in parenthood; for them too, it was the first pregnancy. But they were experts in faith, experts in God, experts in the hope that comes from him; and this is what the world needs in every age. Mary was able to listen to those elderly and amazed parents; she treasured their wisdom, and it proved precious for her in her journey as a woman, as a wife, and as a mother.

The Virgin Mary likewise shows us the way: the way of encounter between the young and the elderly. The future of a people necessarily supposes this encounter: the young give the strength which enables a people to move forward, while the elderly consolidate this strength by their memory and their traditional wisdom.

—HOMILY, ST. PETER'S SQUARE, MASS FOR THE ELDERLY,
SEPTEMBER 28, 2014

3. THE FAITH OF OUR MOTHER
LUKE 1:39-56

Today's page of the Gospel presents to us Mary, who, just after conceiving Jesus through the work of the Holy Spirit, goes to visit her elderly relative Elizabeth, who is also miraculously expecting a child. In this meeting filled with the Holy Spirit, Mary expresses her joy with the Canticle of the Magnificat, because she has become fully aware of the meaning of the great things that are being accomplished in her life: through her, all that her people were expecting is brought to fulfillment.

But the Gospel also shows us the truest cause of Mary's greatness and her blessedness: the cause is faith. Indeed, Elizabeth greets her with these words: "Blessed is she who believed that there would be a fulfilment of what was spoken to her from the Lord" (Luke 1:45). Faith is the heart of Mary's whole story: she is the believer, the great believer; she knows—and she says so—that historically the violence of the powerful, the pride of the rich, the arrogance of the proud are burdensome. However, Mary believes and proclaims that God does not leave his humble and poor children alone but helps them with mercy, with care, over-throwing the mighty from their thrones, scattering the proud in the machinations of their hearts. This is the faith of our Mother, this is the faith of Mary!

The Canticle of Our Lady also enables us to grasp the full meaning of Mary's life: as the mercy of the Lord is the driving force of history, then she could not "know the corruption of the sepulchre, she who begot the Lord of life" (cf. Preface for the

Mass of the Assumption of the Blessed Virgin Mary). All this is not only about Mary. The "great things" [Luke 1:49] done in her by the Almighty touch us deeply, speak to us of our journey in life, remind us of the destination that awaits us: our Father's house. Our life, seen in the light of Mary assumed into heaven, is not a meaningless wandering but is a pilgrimage which, while with all its uncertainty and suffering, has a sure destination: our Father's house, who awaits us with love. It is beautiful to consider this: that we have a Father who waits for us with love, and that our Mother Mary is also up there and waiting for us with love.

Meanwhile, as life goes by, God makes shine "for his pilgrim people on earth, a sign of comfort and sure hope" (cf. Preface). That sign has a face, that sign has a name: the luminous face of the Mother of the Lord, the blessed name of Mary, full of grace, for she believed in the word of the Lord: the great believer! As members of the Church, we are destined to share our Mother's glory because, thanks be to God, we, too, believe in Christ's sacrifice on the cross and, through baptism, we were incorporated into that mystery of salvation.

Today let us all pray together, as our journey on this earth unfolds, that she turn her merciful eyes to us, light the way, point us toward the destination, and show us, after Jesus' exile, the blessed fruit of her womb. And let us say together: O clement, O pious, O sweet Virgin Mary!

—ANGELUS ADDRESS, ST. PETER'S SQUARE, SOLEMNITY OF THE
ASSUMPTION OF THE BLESSED VIRGIN MARY, AUGUST 15, 2015

4. JOSEPH, FAITHFUL AND JUST
MATTHEW 1:18-24

The Gospel tells us about the events preceding the birth of Jesus, and the Evangelist Matthew presents them from the point of view of St. Joseph, the betrothed of the Virgin Mary.

Joseph and Mary were dwelling in Nazareth; they were not yet living together because they were not yet married. In the meantime, Mary, after having welcomed the angel's announcement, came to be with child by the power of the Holy Spirit. When Joseph realized this, he was bewildered. The Gospel does not explain what his thoughts were, but it does tell us the essential: he seeks to do the will of God and is ready for the most radical renunciation. Rather than defending himself and asserting his rights, Joseph chooses what for him is an enormous sacrifice. And the Gospel tells us: "Joseph, being a just man and unwilling to put her to shame, resolved to send her away quietly" (Matthew 1:19).

This brief sentence reveals a true inner drama if we think about the love that Joseph had for Mary! But even in these circumstances, Joseph intends to do the will of God and decides, surely with great sorrow, to send Mary away quietly. We need to meditate on these words in order to understand the great trial that Joseph had to endure in the days preceding Jesus' birth. It was a trial similar to the sacrifice of Abraham, when God asked him for his son Isaac (cf. Genesis 22): to give up what was most precious, the person most beloved.

But as in the case of Abraham, the Lord intervenes: he found the faith he was looking for, and he opens up a different path, a path of love and of happiness. "Joseph," he says, "do not fear to take Mary your wife, for that which is conceived in her is of the Holy Spirit" (Matthew 1:20).

This Gospel passage reveals to us the greatness of St. Joseph's heart and soul. He was following a good plan for his life, but God was reserving another plan for him, a greater mission. Joseph was a man who always listened to the voice of God; he was deeply sensitive to his secret will; he was a man attentive to the messages that came to him from the depths of his heart and from on high.

He did not persist in following his own plan for his life; he did not allow bitterness to poison his soul; rather, he was ready to make himself available to the news that, in such a bewildering way, was being presented to him. And thus, he was a good man. He did not hate, and he did not allow bitterness to poison his soul. Yet how many times does hatred, or even dislike and bitterness, poison our souls! And this is harmful. Never allow it: he is an example of this. And Joseph thereby became even freer and greater. By accepting himself according to God's design, Joseph fully finds himself beyond himself. His freedom to renounce even what is his, the possession of his very life, and his full interior availability to the will of God challenge us and show us the way.

—ANGELUS ADDRESS, ST. PETER'S SQUARE, DECEMBER 22, 2013

5. GOD IS WITH US
JOHN 1:1-14

Once again the liturgy this Sunday sets before us, in the Prologue of the Gospel of St. John, the most profound significance of the birth of Jesus. He is the Word of God who became man and pitched his "tent," his dwelling, among men. The Evangelist writes, "And the Word became flesh and dwelt among us" (John 1:14). These words, that never cease to amaze us, contain the whole of Christianity!

God became mortal, fragile like us; he shared in our human condition except for sin, but he took ours upon himself, as though they were his own. He entered into our history; he became fully God-with-us! The birth of Jesus, then, shows us that God wanted to unite himself to every man and every woman, to every one of us, to communicate to us his life and his joy.

Thus, God is God-with-us, God who loves us, God who walks with us. This is the message of Christmas: the Word became flesh. Thus, Christmas reveals to us the immense love that God has for humanity. From this too derives our enthusiasm, our hope as Christians: that in our poverty we may know that we are loved, that we have been visited, that we are accompanied by God; and we look upon the world and on history as a place in which we walk together with him among us toward a new heaven and a new earth. With the birth of Jesus, a new promise is born; a new world comes into being, but also a world that can be ever renewed.

God is always present to stir up new men, to purify the world of the sin that makes it grow old, from the sin that corrupts it. However much human history and the personal story of each of us may be marked by difficulty and weakness, faith in the Incarnation tells us that God is in solidarity with mankind and with human history. This closeness of God to man, to every man and woman, to each one of us, is a gift that never fades! He is with us! He is God-with-us! Behold the glad tidings of Christmas: the divine light that filled the hearts of the Virgin Mary and St. Joseph and guided the footsteps of the shepherds and the Magi shines today too for us.

In the mystery of the Incarnation of the Son of God, there is also an aspect that is connected to human freedom, to the freedom of each one of us. Indeed, the Word of God pitched his tent among us, sinners who are in need of mercy. And we all must hasten to receive the grace that he offers us. Instead, the Gospel of St. John continues, "His own people received him not" (John 1:11).

We reject him too many times; we prefer to remain closed in our errors and the anxiety of our sins. But Jesus does not desist and never ceases to offer himself and his grace, which save us! Jesus is patient; Jesus knows how to wait; he waits for us always. This is a message of hope, a message of salvation, ancient and ever new. And we are called to witness with joy to this message of the Gospel of life, to the Gospel of light, of hope, and of love. For Jesus' message is this: life, light, hope, and love.

—ANGELUS ADDRESS, ST. PETER'S SQUARE, JANUARY 5, 2014

6. THE TENDERNESS OF GOD
LUKE 2:9, 12

"The people who walked in darkness / have seen a great light; / those who dwelt in a land of deep darkness, / on them has light shined" (Isaiah 9:2). . . .

Isaiah's prophecy announces the rising of a great light which breaks through the night. This light is born in Bethlehem and is welcomed by the loving arms of Mary, by the love of Joseph, by the wonder of the shepherds. When the angels announced the birth of the Redeemer to the shepherds, they did so with these words: "And this will be a sign for you: you will find a babe wrapped in swaddling clothes and lying in a manger" (cf. Luke 2:12).

The "sign" is in fact the humility of God, the humility of God taken to the extreme; it is the love with which, that night, he assumed our frailty, our suffering, our anxieties, our desires, and our limitations. The message that everyone was expecting, that everyone was searching for in the depths of their souls, was none other than the tenderness of God: God who looks upon us with eyes full of love, who accepts our poverty; God who is in love with our smallness.

On this holy night, while we contemplate the Infant Jesus just born and placed in the manger, we are invited to reflect. How do we welcome the tenderness of God? Do I allow myself to be taken up by God, to be embraced by him, or do I prevent him from drawing close? "But I am searching for the Lord," we could respond. Nevertheless, what is most important is not seeking him but rather allowing him to seek me, find me, and caress me with tenderness. The question put to us simply by the Infant's presence is: do I allow God to love me?

More so, do we have the courage to welcome with tenderness the difficulties and problems of those who are near to us, or do we prefer impersonal solutions, perhaps effective but devoid of the warmth of the gospel? How much the world needs tenderness today! The patience of God, the closeness of God, the tenderness of God.

The Christian response cannot be different from God's response to our smallness. Life must be met with goodness, with meekness. When we realize that God is in love with our smallness, that he made himself small in order to better encounter us, we cannot help but open our hearts to him and beseech him: "Lord, help me to be like you; give me the grace of tenderness in the most difficult circumstances of life; give me the grace of closeness in the face of every need, of meekness in every conflict."

—HOMILY, ST. PETER'S BASILICA, MIDNIGHT MASS, SOLEMNITY OF THE NATIVITY OF THE LORD, DECEMBER 24, 2014

7. JESUS ENCOUNTERS EACH OF US
LUKE 2:22-40

The feast of the Presentation of Jesus at the Temple is also known as the feast of the *Encounter*: the liturgy says at the beginning that Jesus goes to meet his people. Thus, this is the encounter *between Jesus and his people*, when Mary and Joseph brought their child to the Temple in Jerusalem; the first encounter between Jesus and his people, represented by Simeon and Anna, took place.

It was also the first encounter within the history of the people, a meeting *between the young and the old*: the young were Mary and Joseph with their infant son, and the old were Simeon and Anna, two people who often went to the Temple.

Let's observe what the Evangelist Luke tells us of them, as he describes them. He says four times that Our Lady and St. Joseph *wanted to do what was required by the law of the Lord* (cf. Luke 2:22, 23, 24, 27). One almost feels and perceives that Jesus' parents have the joy of observing the precepts of God, yes, the joy of walking according to the law of the Lord! They are two newlyweds, they have just had their baby, and they are motivated by the desire to do what is prescribed. This is not an external fact; it is not just to feel right, no! It's a strong desire, a deep desire, full of joy. That's what the psalm says: "In the way of thy testimonies I delight. / . . . For thy law is my delight" (119:14, 77).

And what does St. Luke say of the elderly? He underlines, more than once, that *they were guided by the Holy Spirit*. He

says Simeon was a righteous and devout man, awaiting the con-
solation of Israel, and that "the Holy Spirit was upon him"
(Luke 2:25). He says that "it had been revealed to him by the
Holy Spirit that he should not see death before he had seen the
Lord's Christ" (2:26), and finally, that he went to the Temple
"inspired by the Spirit" (2:27). He says Anna was a "prophet-
ess" (2:36); that is, she was inspired by God and that she was
always "worshiping with fasting and prayer" in the Temple
(2:37). In short, these two elders are full of life! They are full of
life because they are enlivened by the Holy Spirit, obedient to
his action, sensitive to his calls. . . .

And now there is the encounter between the Holy Family and
the two representatives of the holy People of God. Jesus is at the
center. It is he who moves everything, who draws all of them to
the Temple, the house of his Father.

It is a meeting between the young, who are full of joy in
observing the law of the Lord, and the elderly, who are full of
joy in the action of the Holy Spirit. It is *a unique encounter
between observance and prophecy*, where young people are the
observers and the elderly are prophets! In fact, if we think care-
fully, observance of the law is animated by the Spirit, and the
prophecy moves forward along the path traced by the law. Who,
more than Mary, is full of the Holy Spirit? Who more than she
is docile to its action? . . .

It's good for the elderly to communicate their wisdom to the
young; and it's good for the young people to gather this wealth
of experience and wisdom and to carry it forward, not so as to

safeguard it in a museum, but to carry it forward addressing the challenges that life brings, to carry it forward for the sake of the respective religious orders and of the whole Church.

May the grace of this mystery, the mystery of the Encounter, enlighten us and comfort us on our journey. Amen.

—HOMILY, ST. PETER'S BASILICA, FEAST OF THE PRESENTATION,
FEBRUARY 2, 2014

8. LET US SEEK THE LIGHT
MATTHEW 2:1-12

"*Lumen requirunt lumine.*" These evocative words from a liturgical hymn for the Epiphany speak of the experience of the Magi: following a light, they were searching for *the* Light. The star appearing in the sky kindled in their minds and in their hearts a light that moved them to seek the great Light of Christ. The Magi followed faithfully that light which filled their hearts, and they encountered the Lord.

The destiny of every person is symbolized in this journey of the Magi of the East: our life is a journey, illuminated by the lights which brighten our way, to find the fullness of truth and love which we Christians recognize in Jesus, the Light of the World. Like the Magi, every person has two great "books" which provide the signs to guide this pilgrimage: the book of creation and the book of Sacred Scripture. What is important is that we be attentive, alert, and listen to God who speaks to us, who always speaks to us. As the psalm says in referring to the law of the Lord: "Your word is a lamp to my feet and a light to my path" (cf. Psalm 119:105). Listening to the Gospel, reading it, meditating on it, and making it our spiritual nourishment especially allows us to encounter the living Jesus, to experience him and his love.

. . . The Gospel tells us that the Magi, when they arrived in Jerusalem, lost sight of the star for a time. They no longer saw it. Its light was particularly absent from the palace of King Herod: his dwelling was gloomy, filled with darkness, suspicion, fear, envy. Herod, in fact, proved himself distrustful and preoccupied with the birth of a frail child whom he thought of as a rival. In reality, Jesus came not to overthrow him, a wretched puppet, but to overthrow the prince of this world!

Nonetheless, the king and his counselors sensed that the foundations of their power were crumbling. They feared that the rules of the game were being turned upside down, that appearances were being unmasked. A whole world built on power, on success, possessions, and corruption, was being thrown into crisis by a child! Herod went so far as to kill the children. As St. Quodvultdeus writes, "You destroy those who are tiny in body because fear is destroying your heart" (*Sermo 2 de Symbolo: PL 40, 655*). This was in fact the case: Herod was fearful, and on account of this fear, he became insane.

The Magi were able to overcome that dangerous moment of darkness before Herod because they believed the Scriptures, the words of the prophets which indicated that the Messiah would be born in Bethlehem. And so they fled the darkness and dreariness of the night of the world. They resumed their journey toward Bethlehem, and there they once more saw the star, and the Gospel tells us that they experienced "a great joy" (cf. Matthew 2:10)—the very star which could not be seen in that dark, worldly palace.

One aspect of the light which guides us on the journey of faith is holy "cunning." This holy "cunning" is also a virtue. It consists of a spiritual shrewdness which enables us to recognize danger and avoid it. The Magi used this light of "cunning" when, on the way back, they decided not to pass by the gloomy palace of Herod but to take another route. These wise men from the East teach us how not to fall into the snares of darkness and how to defend ourselves from the shadows which seek to envelop our life. By this holy "cunning," the Magi guarded the faith.

We, too, need to guard the faith, guard it from darkness. Many times, however, it is a darkness under the guise of light. This is because the devil, as St. Paul says, disguises himself at times as an angel of light [2 Corinthians 11:14]. And this is where a holy "cunning" is necessary in order to protect the faith, guarding it from those alarmist voices that exclaim, "Listen, today we must do this, or that . . ." Faith, though, is a grace; it is a gift. We are entrusted with the task of guarding it by means of this holy "cunning" and by prayer, love, charity. We need to welcome the light of God into our hearts and, at the same time, to cultivate that spiritual cunning which is able to combine simplicity with astuteness, as Jesus told his disciples: "Be wise as serpents and innocent as doves" (Matthew 10:16).

On the feast of the Epiphany, as we recall Jesus' manifestation to humanity in the face of a child, may we sense the Magi at our side, as wise companions on the way. Their example helps us to lift our gaze toward the star and to follow the great desires of our heart. They teach us not to be content with a life of mediocrity, of "playing it safe," but to let ourselves be attracted always by what is good, true, and beautiful . . . by God, who is all of this, and so much more!

And they teach us not to be deceived by appearances, by what the world considers great, wise, and powerful. We must not stop at that. It is necessary to guard the faith. Today this is of vital importance: to keep the faith. We must press on further, beyond the darkness, beyond the voices that raise alarm, beyond worldliness, beyond so many forms of modernity that exist today. We must press on toward Bethlehem, where, in the simplicity of a dwelling on the outskirts, beside a mother and father full of love and of faith, there shines forth the Sun from on high, the King of the universe. By the example of the Magi, with our little lights, may we seek the Light and keep the faith. May it be so.

—HOMILY, ST. PETER'S BASILICA, SOLEMNITY OF THE EPIPHANY,
JANUARY 6, 2014

9. WELCOME JESUS IN THE FAMILY
LUKE 2:19, 51-52

The Incarnation of the Son of God opens a new beginning in the universal history of man and woman. And this new beginning happens within a family, in Nazareth. Jesus was born in a family. He could have come in a spectacular way, or as a warrior, an emperor. . . . No, no: he is born in a family, in a family. This is important: to perceive, in the nativity, this beautiful scene.

God chose to come into the world in a human family, which he himself formed. He formed it in a remote village on the outskirts of the Roman Empire. Not in Rome, which was the capital of the empire, not in a big city, but on its nearly invisible outskirts, indeed, of little renown. The Gospels also recall this, almost as an expression: "Can anything good come out of Nazareth?" (John 1:46). Perhaps, in many parts of the world, we still talk this way, when we hear the name of some areas on the periphery of a big city. And so, right there, on the outskirts of the great empire, began the most holy and good story of Jesus among men! And that is where this family was.

Jesus dwelt on that periphery for thirty years. The Evangelist Luke summarizes this period like this: Jesus "was obedient to them" (Luke 2:51)—that is, to Mary and Joseph. And someone might say, "But did this God, who comes to save us, waste thirty years there, in that suburban slum?" He wasted thirty years! He wanted this. Jesus' path was in that family—"and his mother kept all these things in her heart. And Jesus increased in wisdom and in stature, and in favor with God and man" (2:51-52).

[Luke's Gospel] does not recount miracles or healing or preaching—he did none in that period—or of crowds flocking; in Nazareth everything seemed to happen "normally," according to the customs of a pious and hardworking Israelite family: they worked, the mother cooked, she did all the housework, ironed shirts . . . all the things mothers do. The father, a carpenter, worked, taught his son the trade. Thirty years. "But what a waste, Father!" God works in mysterious ways. But what was important—there was the family! And this was not a waste! They were great saints: Mary, the most holy woman, immaculate, and Joseph, a most righteous man. . . . The family.

We are certainly moved by the story of how the adolescent Jesus followed the religious calendar of the community and the social duties; in knowing how, as a young worker, he worked with Joseph; and then how he attended the reading of the Scriptures, in praying the psalms, and in so many other customs of daily life. The Gospels, in their sobriety, make no reference to Jesus' adolescence and leave this task to our loving meditation.

Art, literature, music have taken this journey through imagination. It is certainly not difficult to imagine how much mothers could learn from Mary's care for that Son! And how much fathers could glean from the example of Joseph, a righteous man, who dedicated his life to supporting and protecting the child and his wife—his family—in difficult times. Not to mention how much children could be encouraged by the adolescent Jesus to understand the necessity and beauty of cultivating their most profound vocation and of dreaming great dreams! In those thirty years, Jesus cultivated his vocation, for which the Father had sent him. And in that time, Jesus never became discouraged but increased in courage in order to carry his mission forward.

Each Christian family can, first of all—as Mary and Joseph did—welcome Jesus, listen to him, speak with him, guard him, protect him, grow with him; and in this way improve the world. Let us make room in our heart and in our day for the Lord. As Mary and Joseph also did, and it was not easy: how many difficulties they had to overcome! They were not a superficial family; they were not an unreal family. The family of Nazareth urges us to rediscover the vocation and mission of the family, of every family. And what happened in those thirty years in Nazareth can thus happen to us too: in seeking to make love and not hate normal, making mutual help commonplace, not indifference or enmity.

It is no coincidence, then, that "Nazareth" means "She who keeps," as Mary, who—as the Gospel states—"kept all these things in her heart" (Luke 2:51; cf. 2:19). Since then, each time there is a family that keeps this mystery, even if it were on the periphery of the world, the mystery of the Son of God, the mystery of Jesus who comes to save us, the mystery is at work. He comes to save the world. And this is the great mission of the family: to make room for Jesus who is coming, to welcome Jesus in the family, in each member: children, husband, wife, grandparents. . . . Jesus is there. Welcome him there, in order that he may grow spiritually in the family.

—GENERAL AUDIENCE, ST. PETER'S SQUARE, DECEMBER 17, 2014

10. THE HEAVENS ARE OPENED
MARK 1:7-11

At the time that John the Baptist baptizes Jesus, *the heavens opened*. "When he came up out of the water," St. Mark writes, "immediately he saw the heavens opened" (1:10). This brings to mind the dramatic supplication of the prophet Isaiah: "O that thou wouldst rend the heavens and come down" (64:1). This invocation was granted at the event of the baptism of Jesus. Thus ended the time that the "heavens were closed," which had symbolized the separation between God and man as a consequence of sin. Sin distanced us from God and broke the bond between heaven and earth, thereby determining our misery and failures in our lives. The opening of the heavens indicate that God granted his grace in order that the land bear its fruit (cf. Psalm 85:11-12). . . .

With the baptism of Jesus, not only do the heavens open, but God speaks once again, making *his voice resound*: "This is my beloved Son; with whom I am well pleased" (Mark 1:11). The Father's voice proclaims the mystery that is hidden in the Man baptized by the Forerunner.

Then the *Holy Spirit* descends, in the form of a dove: this allows Christ, the Lord's Consecrated One, to inaugurate his mission, which is our salvation. The Holy Spirit: the Great One forgotten in our prayers. We often pray to Jesus, we pray to the Father, especially in the "Our Father," but we do not often pray to the Holy Spirit; is it true? He is the Forgotten One. And we need to ask for his help, his strength, his inspiration.

The Holy Spirit, who has wholly animated the life and mystery of Jesus, is the same Spirit who today guides Christian existence, the existence of men and women who call themselves and want to be Christians. To subject our Christian life and mission, which we have all received in baptism, to the action of the Holy Spirit means finding the apostolic courage necessary to overcome easy worldly accommodations. Christians and communities who are instead "deaf" to the voice of the Holy Spirit, who urges us to bring the gospel to the ends of the earth and of society, also become "mutes" who do not speak and do not evangelize.

But remember this: pray often to the Holy Spirit, that he help us, give us strength, give us inspiration, and enable us to go forward.

—Angelus Address, St. Peter's Square, Feast of the Baptism
of the Lord, January 11, 2015

11. BEHOLD, THE LAMB OF GOD!
JOHN 1:29-34

The Gospel presents us with the scene of the encounter between Jesus and John the Baptist at the River Jordan. The one who recounts it is the eyewitness, John the Evangelist, who before becoming a disciple of Jesus was a disciple of the Baptist, together with his brother James, with Simon and Andrew, all from Galilee, all fishermen.

The Baptist then sees Jesus who is approaching amid the crowd and, inspired from on High, he recognizes in him the One sent by God; he therefore points him out with these words: "Behold, the Lamb of God, who takes away the sin of the world!" (John 1:29).

The verb that is translated as "take away" literally means "to lift up," "to take upon oneself." Jesus came into the world with a precise mission: to liberate it from the slavery of sin by taking on himself the sins of mankind. How? By loving. There is no other way to conquer evil and sin than by the love that leads to giving up one's life for others. In the testimony of John the Baptist, Jesus assumes the features of the Lord's Suffering Servant, who "has borne our grief and carried our sorrows" (cf. Isaiah 53:4) unto death on the cross. He is the true Paschal Lamb, who immerses himself in the river of our sin in order to purify us.

The Baptist sees before him a man who stands in line with sinners to be baptized, though he had no need of it. A man whom God sent into the world as a Lamb to be immolated. In the New Testament, the word "lamb" recurs many times and always in reference to Jesus. This image of the lamb might be surprising; indeed, an animal that is certainly not characterized by strength and robustness takes upon its shoulders such an oppressive weight. The huge mass of evil is removed and taken away by a weak and fragile creature, a symbol of obedience, docility, and defenseless love that ultimately offers itself in sacrifice. The lamb is not a ruler but docile; it is not aggressive but peaceful; it shows no claws or teeth in the face of any attack; rather, it bears it and is submissive. And so is Jesus! So is Jesus, like a lamb.

What does it mean for the Church, for us today, to be disciples of Jesus, the Lamb of God? It means replacing malice with innocence, replacing power with love, replacing pride with humility, replacing status with service. It is good work! We Christians must do this: replace malice with innocence, replace power with love, replace pride with humility, replace status with service. Being disciples of the Lamb means not living like a "besieged citadel," but like a city placed on a hill, open, welcoming, and supportive. It means not assuming closed attitudes, but rather proposing the gospel to everyone, bearing witness by our lives that following Jesus makes us freer and more joyous.

—ANGELUS ADDRESS, ST. PETER'S SQUARE, JANUARY 19, 2014

12. THE WORD OF GOD IS OUR DEFENSE
MATTHEW 4:1-11

Having descended upon him after his baptism in the Jordan, [the Holy Spirit] prompts Jesus to confront Satan openly in the desert for forty days, before beginning his public ministry.

The tempter seeks to divert Jesus from the Father's plan, that is, from the way of sacrifice, of the love that offers itself in expiation, to make him take an easier path, one of success and power. The duel between Jesus and Satan takes place through strong quotations from Sacred Scripture. The devil, in fact, to divert Jesus from the way of the cross, sets before him false messianic hopes: economic well-being, indicated by the ability to turn stones into bread; a dramatic and miraculous style, with the idea of throwing himself down from the highest point of the Temple in Jerusalem and being saved by angels; and lastly, a shortcut to power and dominion, in exchange for an act of adoration to Satan. These are the three groups of temptations, and we, too, know them well!

Jesus decisively rejects all these temptations and reiterates his firm resolve to follow the path set by the Father, without any kind of compromise with sin or worldly logic. Note well how Jesus responds. He does not dialogue with Satan, as Eve had done in the earthly paradise. Jesus is well aware that there can be no dialogue with Satan, for he is cunning. That is why Jesus, instead of engaging in dialogue as Eve had, chooses to take refuge in the word of God and responds with the power of this word. Let us remember this: at the moment of temptation, of our temptations, there is no arguing with Satan; our defense must always be the word of God! And this will save us.

In his replies to Satan, the Lord, using the word of God, reminds us above all that "man shall not live by bread alone, / but by every word that proceeds from the mouth of God" (Matthew 4:4; cf. Deuteronomy 8:3); and this gives us the strength, sustains us in the struggle against a worldly mind-set that would lower man to the level of his primitive needs, causing him to lose hunger for what is true, good, and beautiful, the hunger for God and for his love. Furthermore, he recalls that "it is written, 'You shall not tempt the Lord your God'" (Matthew 4:7), for the way of faith passes also through darkness and doubt, and is nourished by patience and persevering expectation. Lastly, Jesus recalls that "it is written, 'You shall worship the Lord your God, / and him only shall you serve'" (4:10); i.e., we must rid ourselves of idols, of vain things, and build our lives on what is essential.

Jesus' words will then be borne out in his actions. His absolute fidelity to the Father's plan of love will lead him after about three years to the final reckoning with the "prince of this world" (cf. John 16:11), at the hour of his passion and cross, and Jesus will have his final victory, the victory of love!

—ANGELUS ADDRESS, ST. PETER'S SQUARE, MARCH 9, 2014

13. THE GOSPEL IS THE WORD OF LIFE
MARK 1:21-28

This Sunday's Gospel passage presents Jesus, who, with his small community of disciples, enters Capernaum, the city where Peter lived and which was the largest city in Galilee at that time. Jesus goes to that city.

The Evangelist Mark recounts that, since it was the Sabbath, Jesus went straight to the synagogue and began to teach (cf. 1:21). This reminds us of the primacy of the word of God, the word to be listened to, the word to be received, the word to be proclaimed. Arriving in Capernaum, Jesus does not delay proclaiming the gospel, does not think first about the necessary logistics of his small community, does not tarry over the organization. His primary concern is to communicate the word of God with the power of the Holy Spirit. And the people in the synagogue were astonished because Jesus "taught them as one who had authority, and not as the scribes" (1:22).

What does "with authority" mean? It means that in the human words of Jesus, the power of the Word of God could be felt, the authority of God, who is the inspiration of the Sacred Scriptures. And one of the characteristics of the Word of God is that he does what he says. For the Word of God corresponds to his will. We, on the other hand, often speak empty, shallow words, or superfluous words, words that do not coincide with the truth. Instead, the word of God corresponds to the truth; it is united to his will and fulfills what he says.

Indeed, Jesus, after preaching, immediately demonstrates his authority by freeing a man in the synagogue, who was possessed by a demon (cf. Mark 1:23-36). The very divine authority of Christ provoked the reaction of Satan, hidden in that man; Jesus, in his turn, immediately recognized the voice of the evil one and "rebuked him . . . , 'Be silent, and come out of him!'" (1:25). With the power of his word alone, Jesus frees the person from the evil one. And once again those present were amazed: "He commands even the unclean spirits, and they obey him" (1:27). The word of God arouses amazement in us. It has the power to astonish us.

The gospel is the word of life: it does not oppress people; on the contrary, it frees those who are slaves to the many evil spirits of this world: the spirit of vanity, attachment to money, pride, sensuality. . . . The gospel changes the heart, changes life, transforms evil inclinations into good intentions. The gospel is capable of changing people! Therefore it is the task of Christians to spread the redeeming power throughout the world, becoming missionaries and heralds of the word of God.

This is also suggested by today's passage, which closes with a missionary perspective, saying, "His fame"—the fame of Jesus— "spread everywhere throughout all the surrounding region of Galilee" (Mark 1:28). The new doctrine, taught by Jesus with authority, is what the Church takes to the world, along with the effective signs of his presence: the authoritative teaching and the liberating action of the Son of God become words of salvation and gestures expressing the love of the missionary Church.

Always remember that the gospel has the power to change lives! Do not forget this. It is the Good News, which transforms us only when we allow ourselves to be transformed by it. That is why I always ask you to have daily contact with the Gospel, to read it every day: a verse, a passage, to meditate on it and even to take it with you everywhere: in your pocket, in your bag. . . . In other words, to nourish yourself every day with this inexhaustible source of salvation. Do not forget! Read a passage of the Gospel every day. It is the power that changes us, that transforms us: it changes life; it changes the heart.

—ANGELUS ADDRESS, ST. PETER'S SQUARE, FEBRUARY 1, 2015

14. "HEAL THIS WOUND, LORD!"
MARK 1:29-39

This is what Jesus' life was like: "He went throughout all Galilee, preaching in their synagogues and casting out demons" (Mark 1:39). Jesus who preaches and Jesus who heals. The whole day was like this: preaching to the people, teaching the law, teaching the gospel. And the people look for him to listen to him and also because he heals the sick. "That evening, at sundown, they brought to him all who were sick or possessed with demons. . . . And he healed many who were sick with various diseases, and cast out many demons" (1:32, 34). . . .

We could ask ourselves whether we let Jesus preach to us. Each one of us: "Do I let Jesus preach to me, or [do] I know all? Do I listen to Jesus or do I prefer to listen to something else, perhaps people's gossip, or stories?" Listening to Jesus. Listening to Jesus' preaching. "How can I do this, Father? On which TV channel does Jesus speak?" He speaks to you in the Gospel! And this is an attitude that we still do not have: to go to seek the word of Jesus in the Gospel. To always carry a Gospel with us, a small one, or to have one at our fingertips. Five minutes, ten minutes. When I am traveling or when I have to wait . . . , I take the Gospel from my pocket, or from my bag and I read something; or at home. And Jesus speaks to me, Jesus preaches to me there.

It is the word of Jesus. And we have to get accustomed to this: to hear the word of Jesus, to listen to the word of Jesus in the

43

Gospel. To read a passage, think a bit about what it says, what it is saying to me. If I don't feel it is speaking to me, I move to another. But to have this daily contact with the Gospel, to pray with the Gospel, because this way Jesus preaches to me; he says with the Gospel what he wants to tell me. I know people who always carry it, and when they have a little time, they open it, and this way they always find the right word for the moment they are living in. This is the first thing I wanted to say to you: let the Lord preach to you. Listen to the Lord.

And Jesus heals: let yourselves be healed by Jesus. We all have wounds, everyone: spiritual wounds, sins, hostility, jealousy; perhaps we don't say hello to someone: "Ah, he did this to me, I won't acknowledge him anymore." But this needs to be healed! "How do I do it?" Pray and ask that Jesus heal it. It's sad in a family when siblings don't speak to each other for a small matter, because the devil takes a small matter and makes a world of it. Then hostilities go on, oftentimes for many years, and that family is destroyed. Parents suffer because their children don't speak to each other, or one son's wife doesn't speak to the other, and thus, with jealousy, envy . . . The devil sows this. And the only One who casts out demons is Jesus. The only One who heals these matters is Jesus. For this reason I say to each one of you: let yourself be healed by Jesus.

Each one knows where his wounds are. Each one of us has them; we don't have only one: two, three, four, twenty. Each one knows! May Jesus heal those wounds. But for this I must open my heart, in order that he may come. How do I open my heart? By praying. "But Lord, I can't with those people over there. I hate them. They did this, this, and this . . . " "Heal this wound, Lord." If we ask Jesus for this grace, he will do it.

Let yourself be healed by Jesus. Let Jesus heal you. Let Jesus preach to you and let him heal you. This way I can even preach to others, to teach the words of Jesus, because I let him preach to me; and I can also help heal many wounds, the many wounds that there are. But first I have to do it: let him preach to me and heal me.

—Homily, Pastoral Visit to the Roman Parish *San Michele Arcangelo a Pietralata*, February 8, 2015

15. NO ONE IS EXCLUDED FROM SALVATION
MATTHEW 4:12-23

This Sunday's Gospel recounts the beginnings of the public life of Jesus in the cities and villages of Galilee. His mission does not begin in Jerusalem, the religious center and also the social and political center, but in an area on the outskirts, an area looked down upon by the most observant Jews because of the presence in that region of various foreign peoples; that is why the prophet Isaiah calls it "Galilee of the nations" (9:1).

It is a borderland, a place of transit where people of different races, cultures, and religions converge. Thus, Galilee becomes a symbolic place for the gospel to open to all nations. From this point of view, Galilee is like the world of today: the co-presence of different cultures, the necessity for comparison and the necessity of encounter. We, too, are immersed every day in a kind of "Galilee of the nations," and in this type of context we may feel afraid and give in to the temptation to build fences to make us feel safer, more protected. But Jesus teaches us that the Good News, which he brings, is not reserved to one part of humanity; it is to be communicated to everyone. It is a proclamation of joy destined for those who are waiting for it, but also for all those who perhaps are no longer waiting for anything and haven't even the strength to seek and to ask.

Starting from Galilee, Jesus teaches us that no one is excluded from the salvation of God; rather it is from the margins that

God prefers to begin, from the least, so as to reach everyone. He teaches us a method, his method, which also expresses the content, which is the Father's mercy. "Each Christian and every community must discern the path that the Lord points out, but all of us are asked to obey his call to go forth from our own comfort zone in order to reach all the 'peripheries' in need of the light of the Gospel" (Apostolic Exhortation *Evangelii Gaudium,* 20).

Jesus begins his mission not only from a decentralized place, but also among men whom one would call, refer to, as having a "low profile." When choosing his first disciples and future apostles, he does not turn to the schools of scribes and doctors of the law, but to humble people and simple people, who diligently prepare for the coming of the kingdom of God. Jesus goes to call them where they work, on the lakeshore; they are fishermen. He calls them, and they follow him, immediately. They leave their nets and go with him; their life will become an extraordinary and fascinating adventure.

Dear friends, the Lord is calling today too! The Lord passes through the paths of our daily life. Even today, at this moment, here, the Lord is passing through the square. He is calling us to go with him, to work with him for the kingdom of God, in the "Galilee" of our times. May each one of you think: the Lord is passing by today, the Lord is watching me, he is looking at me! What is the Lord saying to me? And if one of you feels that the Lord says to you, "Follow me," be brave, go with the Lord. The Lord never disappoints. Feel in your heart if the Lord is calling you to follow him. Let's let his gaze rest on us, hear his voice, and follow him! "That the joy of the Gospel may reach to the ends of the earth, illuminating even the fringes of our world" (*Evangelii Gaudium*, 288).

—Angelus Address, St. Peter's Square, January 26, 2014

16. COMPASSION: THE TOUCH OF MERCY
MARK 1:40-45

Mark the Evangelist speaks to us about Jesus' actions against every type of evil, for the benefit of those suffering in body and spirit: the possessed, the sick, sinners . . . Jesus presents himself as the One who fights and conquers evil wherever he encounters it. In today's Gospel, this struggle of his confronts an emblematic case, because the sick man is a leper. Leprosy is a contagious and pitiless disease, which disfigures the person, and it was a symbol of impurity: a leper had to stay outside of inhabited centers and make his presence known to passersby. He was marginalized by the civil and religious community. He was like a dead man walking.

The episode of the healing of the leper takes place in three brief phases: the sick man's supplication, Jesus' response, and the result of the miraculous healing. The leper beseeches Jesus, "kneeling," and says to him, "If you will, you can make me clean" (Mark 1:40). Jesus responds to this humble and trusting prayer because his soul is moved to deep pity: *compassion*. "Compassion" is a most profound word: compassion means "to suffer-with-another." Jesus' heart manifests God's paternal compassion for that man, moving close to him and *touching him*. And this detail is very important. Jesus "stretched out his hand and *touched him*. . . . And immediately the leprosy left him, and he was made clean" (1:41, 42).

God's mercy overcomes every barrier, and Jesus' hand touches the leper. He does not stand at a safe distance and does not act by delegating, but places himself in direct contact with our contagion, and in precisely this way our ills become the motive for contact: he, Jesus, takes from us our diseased humanity, and we take from him his sound and healing humanity. This happens each time we receive a sacrament with faith: the Lord Jesus "touches" us and grants us his grace. In this case, we think especially of the Sacrament of Reconciliation, which heals us from the leprosy of sin.

Once again the Gospel shows us what God does in the face of our ills: God does not come to "give a lesson" on pain; neither does he come to eliminate suffering and death from the world; but rather, he comes to take upon himself the burden of our human condition and carries it to the end, to free us in a radical and definitive way. This is how Christ fights the world's maladies and suffering: by taking them upon himself and conquering them with the power of God's mercy.

The Gospel of the healing of the leper tells us today that if we want to be true disciples of Jesus, we are called to become united to him, instruments of his merciful love, overcoming every kind of marginalization. In order to be "imitators of Christ" (cf. 1 Corinthians 11:1) in the face of a poor or sick person, we must not be afraid to look him in the eye and to draw near with tenderness and compassion, and to touch him and embrace him. I have often asked this of people who help others, to do so looking them in the eye, not to be afraid to touch them; that this gesture of help may also be a gesture of communication: we, too, need to be welcomed by them. A gesture of tenderness, a gesture of compassion . . .

Let us ask you: when you help others, do you look them in the eye? Do you embrace them without being afraid to touch them? Do you embrace them with tenderness? Think about this: how do you help? From a distance or with tenderness, with closeness? If evil is contagious, so is goodness. Therefore, there needs to be ever more abundant goodness in us. Let us be infected by goodness and let us spread goodness!

—Angelus Address, St. Peter's Square, February 15, 2015

17. LIVE AS SALT AND LIGHT
MATTHEW 5:13-16

In this Sunday's Gospel passage, immediately after the beatitudes, Jesus says to his disciples, "You are the salt of the earth. . . . You are the light of the world" (Matthew 5:13, 14). This surprises us a bit when we think of those who were before Jesus when he spoke these words. Who were these disciples? They were fishermen, simple people. . . . But Jesus sees them with God's eyes, and his assertion can be understood precisely as a result of the beatitudes. He wishes to say: if you are poor in spirit, if you are meek, if you are pure of heart, if you are merciful . . . you will be the salt of the earth and the light of the world!

To better understand these images, we must keep in mind that Jewish law prescribed that a little bit of salt be sprinkled over every offering presented to God, as a sign of the covenant. Light for Israel was a symbol of messianic revelation, triumph over the darkness of paganism. Christians, the new Israel, receive a mission to carry [this light] into the world for all men: through faith and charity they can guide, consecrate, and make humanity fruitful. We who are baptized Christians are missionary disciples, and we are called to become a living gospel in the world: with a holy life we will "flavor" different environments and defend them from decay, as salt does, and we will carry the light of Christ through the witness of genuine charity.

But if we Christians lose this flavor and do not live as salt and light, we lose our effectiveness. This mission of giving light to the world is so beautiful! We have this mission, and it is beautiful! It is also beautiful to keep the light we have received from Jesus, protecting it and safeguarding it. The Christian should be a luminous person, one who brings light, who always gives off light! A light that is not his, but a gift from God, a gift from Jesus. We carry this light. If a Christian extinguishes this light, his life has no meaning: he is a Christian by name only, who does not carry light; his life has no meaning. I would like to ask you now, how do you want to live? As a lamp that is burning or one that is not? Burning or not? How would you like to live? *[The people respond: Burning!]* As burning lamps! It is truly God who gives us this light, and we must give it to others. Shining lamps! This is the Christian vocation.

—ANGELUS ADDRESS, ST. PETER'S SQUARE, FEBRUARY 9, 2014

18. THE REQUIREMENTS OF LOVE
MATTHEW 5:17-37

This Sunday's Gospel continues the "Sermon on the Mount," Jesus' first great preaching. Today's theme is Jesus' attitude toward the Jewish law. He says, "Think not that I have come to abolish the law and the prophets; I have come not to abolish them but to fulfil them" (Matthew 5:17). Jesus did not want to do away with the commandments that the Lord had given through Moses; rather, he wanted to bring them to fulfillment. He then added that this "fulfillment" of the law requires a higher kind of justice, a more authentic observance. In fact, he says to his disciples, "Unless your righteousness exceeds that of the scribes and Pharisees, you will never enter the kingdom of heaven" (5:20).

But what does this "fulfillment" of the law mean? What is this superior justice? Jesus himself answers this question with a few examples. Jesus was practical, and he always used examples to make himself understood, comparing the old law with his teachings. He begins with the fifth of the Ten Commandments: "You have heard that it was said to the men of old, 'You shalt not kill.' . . . But I say to you that every one who is angry with his brother . . . shall be liable to the council" (Matthew 5:21-22). In this way, Jesus reminds us that words can kill! When we say that a person has the tongue of a snake, what does that mean? That their words kill! Not only is it wrong to take the life of another, but it is also wrong to bestow the poison of anger upon him, strike him with slander, and speak ill of him.

This brings us to gossip: gossip can also kill, because it kills the reputation of the person! It is so terrible to gossip! At first it may seem like a nice thing, even amusing, like enjoying a candy. But in the end, it fills the heart with bitterness, and even poisons us. What I am telling you is true; I am convinced that if each one of us decided to avoid gossiping, we would eventually become holy! What a beautiful path that is! Do we want to become holy? Yes or no? *[The people: Yes!]* Do we want to be attached to the habit of gossip? Yes or no? *[The people: No!]* So we agree then: no gossiping! Jesus offers the perfection of love to those who follow him: love is the only measure that has no measure, to move past judgments.

Love of neighbor is a fundamental attitude that Jesus speaks of, and he says that our relationship with God cannot be honest if we are not willing to make peace with our neighbor. He says, "So if you are offering your gift at the altar, and there remember that your brother has something against you, leave your gift there before the altar and go; first be reconciled to your brother, and then come and offer your gift" (Matthew 5:23-24). Therefore we are called to reconcile with our neighbor before showing our devotion to the Lord in prayer.

In all of this, we see that Jesus does not give importance simply to disciplinary compliance and exterior conduct. He goes to the law's roots, focusing, first and foremost, on the intention and the human heart, from which our good and bad actions originate. To obtain good and honest conduct, legal rules are not enough. We need a deep motivation, an expression of a hidden wisdom, God's wisdom, which can be received through the Holy

Spirit. Through faith in Christ, we can open ourselves to the action of the Spirit, which enables us to experience divine love.

In the light of Christ's teaching, every precept reveals its full meaning as a requirement of love, and they all come together in the greatest commandment: to love God with all of your heart and to love your neighbor as yourself.

—ANGELUS ADDRESS, ST. PETER'S SQUARE, FEBRUARY 16, 2014

19. THE SEED OF THE DIVINE WORD
MARK 4:26-34

Today's Gospel is composed of two very brief parables: that of the seed that sprouts and grows on its own, and that of the mustard seed. Through these images taken from the rural world, Jesus presents the efficacy of the word of God and the requirements of his kingdom, showing the reasons for our hope and our commitment in history.

In the first parable, attention is placed on the fact that the seed scattered on the ground (Mark 4:26) *takes root and develops on its own*, regardless of whether the farmer sleeps or keeps watch. He is confident in the inner power of the seed itself and in the fertility of the soil. In the language of the Gospel, the seed is the symbol of the word of God, whose fruitfulness is recalled in this parable. As the humble seed grows in the earth, so too does the word, by the power of God, work in the hearts of those who listen to it. God has entrusted his word to our earth, that is, to each one of us with our concrete humanity. We can be confident because the word of God is a creative word, destined to become the "full grain in the ear" (4:28). This word, if accepted, certainly bears fruit, for God himself makes it sprout and grow in ways that we cannot always verify or understand. (cf. 4:27). All this tells us that it is always God, it is always God who makes his kingdom grow. That is why we fervently pray, "Thy kingdom come." It is he who makes it grow. Man is his humble collaborator, who contemplates and rejoices in divine creative action and waits patiently for its fruits.

The word of God makes things grow; it gives life. And here, I would like to remind you once again of the importance of having the Gospel, the Bible, close at hand. A small Gospel in your purse, in your pocket, and to nourish yourselves every day with this living word of God. Read a passage from the Gospel every day, a passage from the Bible. Please don't ever forget this. Because this is the power that makes the life of the kingdom of God sprout within us.

The second parable uses the image of the mustard seed. Despite being *the smallest* of all the seeds, it is full of life and grows until it becomes *"the greatest of all shrubs"* (Mark 4:32). And thus is the kingdom of God: a humanly small and seemingly irrelevant reality. To become a part of it, one must be poor of heart; not trusting in [one's] own abilities, but in the power of the love of God; not acting to be important in the eyes of the world, but precious in the eyes of God, who prefers the simple and the humble. When we live like this, the strength of Christ bursts through us and transforms what is small and modest into a reality that leavens the entire mass of the world and of history.

An important lesson comes to us from these two parables: God's kingdom requires *our cooperation*, but it is above all the *initiative and gift of the Lord*. Our weak effort, seemingly small before the complexity of the problems of the world, when integrated with God's effort, fears no difficulty. The victory of the Lord is certain: *his love will make every seed of goodness present on the ground sprout and grow*. This opens us up to trust and hope, despite the tragedies, the injustices, the sufferings that we encounter. The seed of goodness and peace sprouts and develops because the merciful love of God makes it ripen.

May the Holy Virgin, who like "fertile ground" received the seed of the divine Word, sustain us in this hope which never disappoints.

—ANGELUS ADDRESS, ST. PETER'S SQUARE, JUNE 14, 2015

20. THE NEW WINE
JOHN 2:1-11

The Gospel passage which we have just heard is the first momentous sign in the Gospel according to John. Mary's maternal concern is seen in her plea to Jesus: "They have no wine" (John 2:3), and Jesus' reference to his "hour" will be more fully understood later, in the story of his passion.

And this is good, because it allows us to see Jesus' eagerness to teach, to accompany, to heal, and to give joy, thanks to the words of his mother: "They have no wine."

The wedding at Cana is repeated in every generation, in every family, in every one of us and our efforts to let our hearts find rest in strong love, fruitful love, and joyful love. Let us make room for Mary, "the mother" as the Evangelist calls her [John 2:1, 3]. Let us journey with her now to Cana.

Mary is attentive; she is attentive in the course of this wedding feast; she is concerned for the needs of the newlyweds. She is not closed in on herself, worried only about her little world. Her love makes her "outgoing" toward others. She does not seek her friends to say what is happening, to criticize the poor organization of the wedding feast. And since she is attentive, she discreetly notices that the wine has run out. Wine is a sign of happiness, love, and plenty. How many of our adolescents and young people sense that there is no longer any of that wine to be found in their homes? How many women, sad and lonely, wonder when love left, when it slipped away from their lives? How many elderly people feel left out of family celebrations, cast aside and longing each day for a little love, from their sons and daughters, their grandchildren, their great-grandchildren? . . .

But Mary, at the very moment she perceives that there is no wine, approaches Jesus with confidence: this means that *Mary prays*. She goes to Jesus, she prays. She does not go to the steward; she immediately tells her son of the newlyweds' problem. The response she receives seems disheartening: "What does it have to do with you and me? My hour has not yet come" (cf. John 2:4). But she nonetheless places the problem in God's hands. Her deep concern to meet the needs of others hastens Jesus' hour. . . .

Praying always lifts us out of our worries and concerns. It makes us rise above everything that hurts, upsets, or disappoints us and helps to put ourselves in the place of others, in their shoes. The family is a school where prayer also reminds us that we are not isolated individuals; we are one and we have a neighbor close at hand: he or she is living under the same roof, is a part of our life, and is in need.

And finally, *Mary acts*. Her words, "Do whatever he tells you" (John 2:5), addressed to the attendants, are also an invitation to us to open our hearts to Jesus, who came to serve and not to be served. Service is the sign of true love. Those who love know how to serve others. We learn this especially in the family, where we become servants out of love for one another. In the heart of the family, no one is rejected; all have the same value. . . .

In the family, and we are all witnesses of this, miracles are performed with what little we have, with what we are, with what is at hand . . . and many times, it is not ideal, it is not what we dreamt of, nor what "should have been." There is one detail that makes us think: the new wine, that good wine mentioned by the steward at the wedding feast of Cana, came from the water jars, the jars used for ablutions; we might even say from the place where everyone had left their sins . . . it came from the "worst" because "where sin increased, grace abounded all the more" (Romans 5:20). In our own families and in the greater family to which we all belong, nothing is thrown away; nothing is useless. . . .

All this began because "they had no wine." It could all be done because a woman—the Virgin Mary—was attentive, left her concerns in God's hands, and acted sensibly and courageously. But there is a further detail; the best was to come: everyone went on to enjoy the finest of wines. And this is the Good News: the finest wines are yet to be tasted; for families, the richest, deepest, and most beautiful things are yet to come. The time is coming when we will taste love daily, when our children will come to appreciate the home we share, and our elderly will be present each day in the joys of life.

The finest of wines is expressed by hope: this wine will come for every person who stakes everything on love. And the best wine is yet to come, in spite of all the variables and statistics which say otherwise. The best wine will come to those who today feel hopelessly lost. Say it to yourselves until you are convinced of it. Say it to yourselves, in your hearts: the best wine is yet to come. Whisper it to the hopeless and the loveless. Have patience, hope, and follow Mary's example: pray, open your heart, because the best wine is yet to come. God always seeks out the peripheries, those who have run out of wine, those who drink only of discouragement. Jesus feels their weakness, in order to pour out the best wines for those who, for whatever reason, feel that all their jars have been broken.

As Mary bids us, let us "do what the Lord tells us." Do what he tells you. And let us be thankful that in this, our time and our hour, the new wine, the finest wine, will make us recover the joy of families, the joy of living in a family. Let it be so.

—Homily, Guayaquil, Ecuador, July 6, 2015

21. "CLEANSE US, JESUS, WITH YOUR MERCY"

John 2:13-25

In the Gospel passage that we heard, there are two things that strike me: an image and a word. The image is that of Jesus, with whip in hand, driving out all those who took advantage of the Temple to do business. These profiteers who sold animals for sacrifices, changed coins. There was the sacred—the Temple, sacred—and this filth, outside. This is the image. And Jesus takes the whip and goes forth, to somewhat cleanse the Temple.

And the phrase, the word, is there where it says that so many people believe in him, a horrible phrase: "But Jesus did not trust himself to them, because he knew all men and needed no one to bear witness of man; for he himself knew what was in man" (John 2:24-25).

We cannot deceive Jesus. He knows us from within. He did not trust them. He, Jesus, did not trust them. And this can be a fine mid-Lenten question: can Jesus trust himself to me? Can Jesus trust me, or am I two-faced? Do I play the Catholic, one close to the Church, and then live as a pagan? "But Jesus doesn't know; no one goes and tells him about it." He knows. "He needed no one to bear witness; indeed, he knew what was in man." Jesus knows all that there is in our heart. We cannot deceive Jesus. In front of him we cannot pretend to be saints, and close our eyes, act like this, and then live a life that is not what he wants. And he knows. And we all know the name he gave to those who had two faces: hypocrites.

It will do us good today to enter our hearts and look at Jesus. To say to him, "Lord, look, there are good things, but there are also things that aren't good. Jesus, do you trust me? I am a sinner . . ." This doesn't scare Jesus. If you tell him, "I'm a sinner," it doesn't scare him. What distances him is one who is two-faced: showing him/herself as just in order to cover up hidden sin. "But I go to church every Sunday, and I . . ." Yes, we can say all of this. But if your heart isn't just, if you don't do justice, if you don't love those who need love, if you do not live according to the spirit of the beatitudes, you are not Catholic. You are a hypocrite. First: can Jesus trust himself to me? In prayer, let us ask him: Lord, do you trust me?

Second, the gesture. When we enter our hearts, we find things that aren't okay, things that aren't good, as Jesus found that filth of profiteering, of the profiteers, in the Temple. Inside of us too, there are unclean things; there are sins of selfishness, of arrogance, pride, greed, envy, jealousy . . . so many sins! We can even continue the dialogue with Jesus: "Jesus, do you trust me? I want you to trust me. Thus I open the door to you, and you cleanse my soul." Ask the Lord that, as he went to cleanse the Temple, he may come to cleanse your soul.

We imagine that he comes with a whip of cords. No, he doesn't cleanse the soul with that! Do you know what kind of whip Jesus uses to cleanse our soul? Mercy. Open your heart to

Jesus' mercy! Say, "Jesus, look how much filth! Come, cleanse. Cleanse with your mercy, with your tender words, cleanse with your caresses." If we open our heart to Jesus' mercy, in order to cleanse our heart, our soul, Jesus will trust himself to us.

—HOMILY, PASTORAL VISIT TO THE ROMAN PARISH *SANTA MARIA MADRE DEL REDENTORE A TOR BELLA MONACA*, MARCH 8, 2015

22. THIRSTING FOR JESUS
JOHN 4:5-42

Today's Gospel presents Jesus' encounter with the Samaritan woman in Sychar, near an old well where the woman went to draw water daily. That day she found Jesus seated, "wearied as he was with his journey" (John 4:6). He immediately says to her, "Give me a drink" (4:7). In this way he overcomes the barriers of hostility that existed between Jews and Samaritans and breaks the mold of prejudice against women.

This simple request from Jesus is the start of a frank dialogue, through which he enters with great delicacy into the interior world of a person to whom, according to social norms, he should not have spoken. But Jesus does! Jesus is not afraid. When Jesus sees a person, he goes ahead, because he loves. He loves us all. He never hesitates before a person out of prejudice. Jesus sets her own situation before her, not by judging her, but by making her feel worthy, acknowledged, and thus arousing in her the desire to go beyond the daily routine.

Jesus' thirst was not so much for water but for the encounter with a parched soul. Jesus needed to encounter the Samaritan woman in order to open her heart: he asks for a drink so as to bring to light her own thirst. The woman is moved by this encounter: she asks Jesus several profound questions that we all carry within but often ignore. We, too, have many questions to ask, but we don't have the courage to ask Jesus! Lent, dear brothers and sisters, is the opportune time to look within ourselves, to understand our truest spiritual needs, and to ask the

Lord's help in prayer. The example of the Samaritan woman invites us to exclaim, "Jesus, give me a drink that will quench my thirst forever."

The Gospel says that the disciples marveled that their master was speaking to this woman. But the Lord is greater than prejudice, which is why he was not afraid to address the Samaritan woman: mercy is greater than prejudice. We must learn this well! Mercy is greater than prejudice, and Jesus is so very merciful, very!

The outcome of that encounter by the well was the woman's transformation: "The woman left her water jar" (John 4:28), with which she had come to draw water, and ran to the city to tell people about her extraordinary experience. "I found a man who told me all that I ever did. Can this be the Christ?" (cf. 4:29). She was excited. She had gone to draw water from the well, but she found another kind of water, the living water of mercy from which gushes forth eternal life. She found the water she had always sought!

She runs to the village, that village which had judged her, condemned her, and rejected her, and she announces that she has met the Messiah: the one who has changed her life. Because every encounter with Jesus changes our lives, always. It is a step forward, a step closer to God. And thus every encounter with Jesus changes our life. It is always, always this way.

In this Gospel passage, we likewise find the impetus to "leave behind our water jar," the symbol of everything that is seemingly important but loses all its value before the "love of God." We all have one, or more than one! I ask you, and myself: "What is your interior water jar, the one that weighs you down, that distances you from God?" Let us set it aside a little, and with our hearts let us hear the voice of Jesus offering us another kind of water, another water that brings us close to the Lord.

We are called to rediscover the importance and the sense of our Christian life, initiated in baptism, and, like the Samaritan woman, to witness to our brothers. A witness of what? Joy! To witness to the joy of the encounter with Jesus; for, as I said, every encounter with Jesus changes our life, and every encounter with Jesus also fills us with joy, the joy that comes from within. And the Lord is like this. And so we must tell of the marvelous things the Lord can do in our hearts when we have the courage to set aside our own water jar.

—Angelus Address, St. Peter's Square, March 23, 2014

23. "DO NOT FEAR, ONLY BELIEVE"
MARK 5:21-43

Today's Gospel presents the account of the resurrection of a young twelve-year-old girl, the daughter of one of the leaders of the synagogue, who falls at Jesus' feet and beseeches him: "My little daughter is at the point of death. Come and lay your hands on her, so that she may be made well, and live" (Mark 5:23). In this prayer we hear the concern of every father for the life and well-being of his child.

We also hear the great faith which that man has in Jesus. And when news arrives that the little girl is dead, Jesus tells him, "Do not fear, only believe" (Mark 5:36). These words from Jesus give us courage! And he frequently also says them to us: "Do not fear, only believe." Entering the house, the Lord sends away all those who are weeping and wailing and turns to the dead girl, saying, "Little girl, I say to you, arise" (5:41). And immediately the little girl rose and began to walk. Here we see Jesus' absolute power over death, which for him is like a dream from which one can awaken.

The Evangelist inserts another episode in this account: the healing of a woman who had been bleeding for twelve years. Because of this ailment, which, according to the culture of the time, rendered her "impure," she was forced to avoid all human contact. The poor woman was condemned to a civic death. In the midst of the crowd following Jesus, this unknown woman says to herself, "If I touch even his garments, I shall be made well" (Mark 5:28). And thus it happened. The need to be freed urges her to dare, and her faith "snatches," so to speak, healing from the Lord. She who believes "touches" Jesus and draws from him a saving grace.

This is faith: to touch Jesus is to draw from him the grace that saves. It saves us, it saves our spiritual life, it saves us from so many problems. Jesus notices and, in the midst of the people, looks for the woman's face. She steps forward, trembling, and he says to her, "Daughter, your faith has made you well" (Mark 5:34). It is the voice of the heavenly Father who speaks in Jesus: "Daughter, you are not cursed, you are not excluded, you are my child!" And every time Jesus approaches us, when we go forth from him with faith, we feel this from the Father: "Child, you are my son, you are my daughter! You are healed. I forgive everyone for everything. I heal all people and all things."

These two episodes—a healing and a resurrection—share one core: *faith*. The message is clear, and it can be summed up in one question: *do we believe that Jesus can heal us and can raise us from the dead*? The entire gospel is written in the light of this faith: Jesus is risen, he has conquered death, and by his victory we, too, will rise again. This faith, which for the first Christians was sure, can tarnish and become uncertain, to the point that some may confuse resurrection with reincarnation.

The word of God invites us to live in the certainty of the resurrection: Jesus is the Lord, Jesus has power over evil and over death, and he wants to lead us to the house of the Father, where life reigns. And there we will all meet again, all of us here in this square today, we will meet again in the house of the Father, in the life that Jesus will give us.

The resurrection of Christ acts in history as the principle of renewal and hope. Anyone who is desperate and tired to death, if he entrusts himself to Jesus and to his love, can begin to live again. And to begin a new life, to change life, is a way of rising again, of resurrecting. Faith is a force of life; it gives fullness to our humanity; and those who believe in Christ must acknowledge this in order to promote life in every situation, in order to let everyone, especially the weakest, experience the love of God who frees and saves.

—ANGELUS ADDRESS, ST. PETER'S SQUARE, JUNE 28, 2015

24. THE LANGUAGE OF HOSPITALITY
Mark 6:7-13

The Gospel speaks to us of . . . discipleship. It shows us the identity card of the Christian. Our calling card, our credentials.

Jesus calls his disciples and sends them out, giving them clear and precise instructions. He challenges them to take on a whole range of attitudes and ways of acting. Sometimes these can strike us as exaggerated or even absurd. It would be easier to interpret these attitudes symbolically or "spiritually." But Jesus is quite precise, very clear. He doesn't tell them simply to do whatever they think they can.

Let us think about some of these attitudes: "Take nothing for the journey except a staff; no bread, no bag, no money. . . . When you enter a house, stay there until you leave the place" (cf. Mark 6:8, 10). All this might seem quite unrealistic.

We could concentrate on the words "bread," "money," "bag," "staff," "sandals," and "tunic." And this would be fine. But it strikes me that one key word can easily pass unnoticed among the challenging words I have just listed. It is a word at the heart of Christian spirituality, of our experience of discipleship: "welcome." Jesus as the good master, the good teacher, sends them out to be welcomed, to experience hospitality. He says to them, "Where you enter a house, stay there." He sends them out to learn one of the hallmarks of the community of believers. We might say that a Christian is someone who has learned to welcome others, who has learned to show hospitality.

Jesus does not send them out as men of influence, landlords, or officials armed with rules and regulations. Instead, he makes them see that the Christian journey is simply about changing hearts—one's own heart, first of all, and then helping to transform the hearts of others. It is about learning to live differently, under a different law, with different rules. It is about turning from the path of selfishness, conflict, division, and superiority, and taking instead the path of life, generosity, and love. It is about passing from a mentality which domineers, stifles, and manipulates to a mentality which welcomes, accepts, and cares.

These are two contrasting mentalities, two ways of approaching our life and our mission.

How many times do we see mission in terms of plans and programs? How many times do we see evangelization as involving any number of strategies, tactics, maneuvers, techniques, as if we could convert people on the basis of our own arguments? Today the Lord says to us quite clearly: in the mentality of the gospel, you do not convince people with arguments, strategies, or tactics. You convince them by simply learning how to welcome them.

The Church is a mother with an open heart. She knows how to welcome and accept, especially those in need of greater care, those in greater difficulty. The Church, as desired by Jesus, is the home of hospitality. And how much good we can do, if only we try to speak this language of hospitality, this language of receiving and welcoming. How much pain can be soothed, how much despair can be allayed, in a place where we feel at home!

This requires open doors, especially the doors of our heart. Welcoming the hungry, the thirsty, the stranger, the naked, the sick, the prisoner (Matthew 25:34-37), the leper, and the paralytic. Welcoming those who do not think as we do, who do not have faith or who have lost it. And sometimes, we are to blame. Welcoming the persecuted, the unemployed. Welcoming the different cultures, of which our earth is so richly blessed. Welcoming sinners, because each one of us is also a sinner.

—Homily, Campo Grande in Ñu Guazú, Asunción, Paraguay,
July 12, 2015

25. TO SEE, TO HAVE COMPASSION, TO TEACH
MARK 6:30-34

Today's Gospel tells us that the apostles, after the experience of the mission, have returned content but also tired. Jesus, filled with understanding, wants to give them some relief; and so he takes them away, to a lonely place, so they can rest a while (cf. Mark 6:31). "Many saw them going, and knew . . . and got there ahead of them" (6:33).

From this point the Evangelist offers us the image of Jesus of singular intensity, "photographing," so to speak, [with] his eyes and gathering the sentiments of his heart. The Evangelist states, "As he landed he saw a great throng, and he had compassion on them, because they were like sheep without a shepherd; and he began to teach them many things" (6:34).

Let us recall the three verbs in this evocative photograph: to see, to have compassion, to teach. We can call them the *verbs of the Shepherd.*

To see, to have compassion, to teach. The first and second, *to see* and *to have compassion,* are always found together in the attitude of Jesus: in fact, his gaze is not the gaze of a sociologist or a photojournalist, for he always gazes with "the eyes of the heart." These two verbs, *to see* and *to have compassion,* configure Jesus as the Good Shepherd. His compassion, too, is not merely a human feeling but is the deep emotion of the Messiah in whom God's tenderness is made flesh.

From this tenderness is born Jesus' wish to nourish the crowd with the bread of his word, that is, to teach the word of God to the people. Jesus sees, Jesus has compassion, Jesus teaches us. This is beautiful!

—ANGELUS ADDRESS, ST. PETER'S SQUARE, JULY 19, 2015

26. GOD'S MERCY IS FOR EVERYONE
LUKE 7:36-50

The Gospel we have heard opens to us a path of hope and comfort. It is good to feel Jesus' compassionate gaze upon us, just as it was felt by the sinful woman in the house of the Pharisee. In this passage, two words persistently return: *love* and *judgment*.

There is *the love of the sinful woman* who humbles herself before the Lord, but before that is *the merciful love of Jesus* for her, which drives her to approach him. Her tears of repentance and joy wash the feet of the Master, and her hair dries them with gratitude; the kisses are an expression of her pure love, and the perfumed ointment poured in abundance attests to how precious he is in her eyes. This woman's every gesture speaks of love and expresses her desire to have unwavering certitude in her life: that of having been forgiven.

And this certitude is beautiful! And Jesus gives her this certitude: in accepting her he demonstrates the love God has for her, just for her, a public sinner! Love and forgiveness are simultaneous: God forgives her many sins. He forgives her for all of them, for "she loved much" (Luke 7:47), and she adores Jesus because she feels that in him there is mercy and not condemnation. She feels that Jesus understands her with love, she who is a sinner. Thanks to Jesus, God lifts her many sins off her shoulders; he no longer remembers them (cf. Isaiah 43:25). For this is also true: when God forgives, he forgets. God's forgiveness is great! For her now a new era begins; through love she is reborn into a new life.

This woman has truly encountered the Lord. In silence she opened her heart; in sorrow she showed repentance for her sins; by her tears she appealed to divine goodness to receive forgiveness. For her there will be no judgment but that which comes from God, and this is the judgment of mercy. The hero of this encounter is certainly love: a mercy which goes beyond justice.

Simon, the master of the house, the Pharisee, on the contrary, *doesn't manage to find the road of love.* Everything is calculated, everything is thought out. . . . He stands firm on the threshold of formality. It is an unpleasant thing, formal love; he doesn't understand. He is not capable of taking that next step forward to meet Jesus who will bring him salvation. Simon limits himself to inviting Jesus to lunch, but did not truly welcome him.

In his thoughts Simon invokes only justice, and, in doing so, he errs. *His judgment of the woman distances him from the truth* and prevents him from even understanding who his guest is. He stopped at the surface—at formality—incapable of seeing the heart. Before the parable of Jesus and the question of which servant would love more, the Pharisee responds correctly: "The one, I suppose, to whom he forgave more." Jesus doesn't fail to observe, "You have judged rightly" (Luke 7:43). When Simon's judgment is turned to love, then is he in the right.

Jesus' reminder urges each of us never to stop at the surface of things, especially when we have a person before us. We are called to look beyond, *to focus on the heart,* in order to see how much generosity everyone is capable of. No one can be excluded from the mercy of God; everyone knows the way to access it, and the Church is the *house where everyone is welcomed and no one is rejected*. Her doors remain wide open, so that those who are touched by grace may find the assurance of forgiveness. The greater the sin, the greater the love that must be shown by the Church to those who repent. With how much love Jesus looks at us!

—Homily, St. Peter's Basilica, Celebration of Penance,
March 13, 2015

27. JESUS, PERFECT ICON OF THE FATHER
MARK 9:2-10

The Gospel recounts the event of the transfiguration, which takes place at the height of Jesus' public ministry. He is on his way to Jerusalem, where the prophecies of the "Servant of God" and his redemptive sacrifice are to be fulfilled. The crowds did not understand this: presented with a Messiah who contrasted with their earthly expectations, they abandoned him. They thought the Messiah would be the liberator from Roman domination, the emancipator of the homeland, and they do not like Jesus' perspective, and so they leave him.

Neither do the apostles understand the words with which Jesus proclaims the outcome of his mission in the glorious passion; they do not understand! Jesus thus chooses to give to Peter, James, and John a foretaste of his glory, which he will have after the resurrection, in order to confirm them in faith and encourage them to follow him on the trying path, on the way of the cross. Thus, on a high mountain, immersed in prayer, he is transfigured before them: his face and his entire person irradiate a blinding light. The three disciples are frightened, as a cloud envelops them and the Father's voice sounds from above, as at the baptism on the Jordan: "This is my beloved Son; listen to him" (Mark 9:7). Jesus is the Son-made-servant, sent into the world to save us all through the cross, fulfilling the plan of salvation. His full adherence to God's will renders his *humanity transparent to the glory of God, who is love.*

Jesus thus reveals himself as the perfect icon of the Father, the radiance of his glory. He is the fulfillment of revelation; that is why beside him Moses and Elijah appear transfigured; they represent the law and the prophets, so as to signify that everything finishes and begins in Jesus, in his passion and in his glory.

Their instructions for the disciples and for us is this: "Listen to him!" Listen to Jesus. He is the Savior: follow him. To listen to Christ, in fact, entails *taking up the logic of his paschal mystery,* setting out on the journey with him to make of oneself a gift of love to others, in docile obedience to the will of God, with an attitude of detachment from worldly things and of interior freedom. One must, in other words, be willing to "lose one's very life" (cf. Mark 8:35) by giving it up so that all men might be saved: thus, we will meet in eternal happiness. The path to Jesus always leads us to happiness; don't forget it! Jesus' way always leads us to happiness. There will always be a cross, trials in the middle, but at the end we are always led to happiness. Jesus does not deceive us; he promised us happiness and will give it to us if we follow his ways.

With Peter, James, and John, we, too, climb the Mount of the Transfiguration today and stop in contemplation of the face of Jesus to retrieve the message and translate it into our lives; for we, too, can be transfigured by Love. In reality, love is capable of transfiguring everything. Love transfigures all! Do you believe this? May the Virgin Mary . . . sustain us on this journey.

—ANGELUS ADDRESS, ST. PETER'S SQUARE, MARCH 1, 2015

28. AN EXCHANGE OF GLANCES
MATTHEW 9:9-13

We are celebrating the feast of the Apostle and Evangelist St. Matthew. We are celebrating the story of a conversion. Matthew himself, in his Gospel, tells us what it was like, this encounter which changed his life. He shows us an "exchange of glances" capable of changing history.

On a day like any other, as Matthew the tax collector was seated at his table, Jesus passed by, saw him, came up to him, and said, "Follow me" (Matthew 9:9). Matthew got up and followed him.

Jesus looked at him. How strong was the love in that look of Jesus, which moved Matthew to do what he did! What power must have been in his eyes to make Matthew get up from his table! We know that Matthew was a publican: he collected taxes from the Jews to give to the Romans. Publicans were looked down upon and considered sinners; for that reason they lived apart and were despised by others. One could hardly eat, speak, or pray with the likes of these. For the people, they were traitors: they extorted from their own to give to others. Publicans belonged to this social class.

Jesus stopped; he did not quickly turn away. He looked at Matthew calmly, peacefully. He looked at him with eyes of mercy; he looked at him as no one had ever looked at him before. And that look unlocked Matthew's heart; it set him free, it healed him, it gave him hope, a new life, as it did to Zacchaeus, to Bartimaeus, to Mary Magdalene, to Peter, and to each of us.

Even if we dare not raise our eyes to the Lord, he always looks at us first. This is our story, and it is like that of so many others. Each of us can say, "I, too, am a sinner, whom Jesus has looked upon." I ask you today, in your homes or at church, when you are alone and at peace, to take a moment to recall with gratitude and happiness those situations, that moment, when the merciful gaze of God was felt in our lives.

Jesus' love goes before us; his look anticipates our needs. He can see beyond appearances, beyond sin, beyond failures and unworthiness. He sees beyond our rank in society. He sees beyond all of this. He sees our dignity as sons and daughters, a dignity at times sullied by sin, but one which endures in the depth of our soul. It is our dignity as sons and daughters. He came precisely to seek out all those who feel unworthy of God, unworthy of others. Let us allow Jesus to look at us. Let us allow his gaze to run over our streets. Let us allow that look to become our joy, our hope, our happiness in life.

After the Lord looked upon him with mercy, he said to Matthew, "Follow me." Matthew got up and followed him. After the look, a word. After love, the mission. Matthew is no longer the same; he is changed inside. The encounter with Jesus and his loving mercy transformed him. His table, his money, his exclusion were all left behind. Before, he had sat waiting to collect his taxes, to take from others; now, with Jesus he must get up and give, give himself to others. Jesus looks at him and Matthew encounters the joy of service. For Matthew and for all who have felt the gaze of Jesus, other people are no longer to be "lived off [of]," used and abused. The gaze of Jesus gives rise to missionary activity, service, self-giving. Other people are those whom Jesus serves. His love heals our shortsightedness and pushes us to look beyond, not to be satisfied with appearances or with what is politically correct.

Jesus goes before us, he precedes us; he opens the way and invites us to follow him. He invites us slowly to overcome our preconceptions and our reluctance to think that others, much less ourselves, can change. He challenges us daily with a question: "Do you believe? Do you believe it is possible that a tax collector can become a servant? Do you believe it is possible that a traitor can become a friend? Do you believe it is possible that the son of a carpenter can be the Son of God?" His gaze transforms our way of seeing things; his heart transforms our hearts. God is a Father who seeks the salvation of each of his sons and daughters.

Let us gaze upon the Lord in prayer, in the Eucharist, in Confession, in our brothers and sisters, especially those who feel excluded or abandoned. May we learn to see them as Jesus sees us. Let us share his tenderness and mercy with the sick, prisoners, the elderly, and families in difficulty. Again and again we are called to learn from Jesus, who always sees what is most authentic in every person, which is the image of his Father.

—HOMILY, MASS AT THE PLAZA DE LA REVOLUCIÓN, HOLGUÍN, CUBA,
FEAST OF ST. MATTHEW, SEPTEMBER 21, 2015

29. CALLED TO SERVE
MARK 9:30-37

Jesus asks his disciples an apparently indiscreet question: "What were you discussing along the way?" [cf. Mark 9:33]. It is a question which he could also ask each of us today: "What do you talk about every day?" "What are your aspirations?" The Gospel tells us that the disciples "did not answer because on the way they had been arguing about who was the most important" (cf. 9:34). They were ashamed to tell Jesus what they were talking about. Like the disciples then, today we, too, can be caught up in these same arguments: who is the most important?

Jesus does not press the question. He does not force them to tell him what they were talking about on the way. But the question lingers, not only in the minds of the disciples, but also in their hearts. . . .

Who is the most important? Jesus is straightforward in his reply: "Whoever wishes to be the first—the most important—among you must be the last of all, and the servant of all" (cf. Mark 9:35). Whoever wishes to be great must serve others, not be served by others.

This is the great paradox of Jesus. The disciples were arguing about who would have the highest place, who would be chosen for privileges—they were the disciples, those closest to Jesus, and they were arguing about that!—who would be above the common law, the general norm, in order to stand out in the quest for superiority over others. Who would climb the ladder most quickly to take the jobs which carry certain benefits.

Jesus upsets their "logic," their mind-set, simply by telling them that life is lived authentically in a concrete commitment to our neighbor. That is, by serving.

The call to serve involves something special, to which we must be attentive. Serving means caring for their vulnerability. Caring for the vulnerable of our families, our society, our people. Theirs are the suffering, fragile, and downcast faces which Jesus tells us specifically to look at and which he asks us to love. With a love which takes shape in our actions and decisions. With a love which finds expression in whatever tasks we, as citizens, are called to perform. It is people of flesh and blood, people with individual lives and stories, and with all their frailty, that Jesus asks us to protect, to care for, and to serve. Being a Christian entails promoting the dignity of our brothers and sisters, fighting for it, living for it. That is why Christians are constantly called to set aside their own wishes and desires, their pursuit of power, before the concrete gaze of those who are most vulnerable.

There is a kind of "service" which serves others, yet we need to be careful not to be tempted by another kind of service, one which is "self-serving" with regard to others. There is a way to go about serving which is interested in only helping "my people," "our people." This service always leaves "your people" outside, and gives rise to a process of exclusion.

All of us are called by virtue of our Christian vocation to that service which truly serves, and to help one another not to be tempted by a "service" which is really "self-serving." All of us are asked, indeed urged by Jesus to care for one another out of love. Without looking to one side or the other to see what our neighbor is doing or not doing. Jesus says, "Whoever would be first among you must be the last, and the servant of all." That person will be the first. Jesus does not say: if your neighbor wants to be first, let him be the servant! We have to be careful to avoid judgmental looks and renew our belief in the transforming look to which Jesus invites us.

This caring for others out of love is not about being servile. Rather, it means putting the question of our brothers and sisters at the center. Service always looks to their faces, touches their flesh, senses their closeness, and even, in some cases, "suffers" that closeness and tries to help them. Service is never ideological, for we do not serve ideas, we serve people. . . .

Let us not forget the Good News we have heard today: the importance of a people, a nation, and the importance of individuals, which is always based on how they seek to serve their vulnerable brothers and sisters. Here we encounter one of the fruits of a true humanity.

Because, dear brothers and sisters: "Whoever does not live to serve, does not 'serve' to live."

—HOMILY, MASS AT THE PLAZA DE LA REVOLUCIÓN, HAVANA, CUBA,

SEPTEMBER 20, 2015

30. LIFE-GIVING BREAD
JOHN 6:51-58

The Gospel of John presents the discourse on the "Bread of Life," held by Jesus in the synagogue of Capernaum, in which he affirms, "I am the living bread come down from heaven; if any one eats of this bread, he will live for ever; and the bread that I shall give for the life of the world is my flesh" (cf. 6:51). Jesus underlines that he has not come into this world to give something but to give himself, his life, as nourishment for those who have faith in him. This, our communion with the Lord, obliges us, his disciples, to imitate him, making our existence, through our behavior, bread broken for others, as the Teacher has broken the bread that is truly his flesh. Instead, this means for us generous conduct toward our neighbor, thereby demonstrating the attitude of giving life for others.

Every time that we participate in Holy Mass and we are nourished by the Body of Christ, the presence of Jesus and of the Holy Spirit acts in us, shaping our hearts, communicating an interior disposition to us that translates into conduct according to the gospel. Above all, docility to the word of God, then fraternity amongst ourselves, the courage of Christian witness, creative charity, the capacity to give hope to the disheartened, to welcome the excluded. In this way, the Eucharist fosters a mature Christian lifestyle.

The charity of Christ, welcomed with an open heart, changes us, transforms us, renders us capable of loving not according to human measure, always limited, but according to the measure of God. And what is the measure of God? Without measure! The measure of God is without measure. Everything! Everything! Everything! It's impossible to measure the love of God: it is without measure! And so we become capable of loving even those who do not love us: and this is not easy.

To love someone who doesn't love us . . . it's not easy! Because if we know that a person doesn't like us, then we also tend to bear ill will. But no! We must love even someone who doesn't love us! Opposing evil with good, with pardon, with sharing, with welcome. Thanks to Jesus and to his Spirit, even our life becomes "bread broken" for our brothers.

And living like this, we discover true joy! The joy of making of oneself a gift, of reciprocating the great gift that we have first received, without merit of our own. This is beautiful: our life is made a gift! This is to imitate Jesus. I wish to remind you of these two things. First, the measure of God's love is love without measure. Is this clear? And our life, with the love of Jesus, received in the Eucharist, is made a gift. As was the life of Jesus. Don't forget these two things: the measure of the love of God is love without measure. And following Jesus, we, with the Eucharist, make of our life a gift.

Jesus, Bread of eternal life, came down from heaven and was made flesh thanks to the faith of Mary Most Holy. After having borne him with ineffable love in herself, she followed him faithfully unto the cross and to the resurrection. Let us ask Our Lady to help us rediscover the beauty of the Eucharist, to make it the center of our life, especially at Sunday Mass and in adoration.

—Angelus Address, St. Peter's Square,
Solemnity of Corpus Christi, June 22, 2014

31. WHO IS JESUS FOR ME?
JOHN 6:60-69

Today the sixth chapter of the Gospel of John concludes with the discourse on the Bread of Life, which Jesus gave the day after the multiplication of the loaves and fish. At the end of that discourse, the great enthusiasm of the previous day had dissipated, for Jesus said that he was the Bread which came down from heaven and that he would give his flesh as food and his blood as drink, thereby clearly alluding to the sacrifice of his life. Those words gave rise to dismay in the people, who deemed such words unworthy of the Messiah, not "winning" words. Thus, several regarded Jesus as a messiah who should have spoken and acted in such a way as to bring success to his mission, straightaway. But they were mistaken precisely in this: in the way of understanding the mission of the Messiah! Not even the disciples managed to accept the unsettling words of the Teacher. And today's passage refers to their discomfort: "This is a hard saying," they commented. "Who can listen to it?" (John 6:60).

In reality, they had certainly understood Jesus' discourse—so well that they did not want to heed it, because it was a discourse which threw their mind-set into crisis. Jesus' words always throw us into crisis—for example, the worldly spirit, worldliness. But Jesus offers the key for overcoming this difficulty, a key consisting of three elements. First, his *divine origin:* he came down from heaven and will ascend again to "where he was before" (John 6:62). Second, his words can be understood only through *the action of the Holy Spirit*. The One who "gives life" (6:63) is precisely the Holy Spirit who enables us to understand Jesus properly. Third, the true cause of incomprehension of his words is the *lack of faith*: "There are some of you that do not believe," Jesus says (6:64). In fact, from that time, the Gospel says, "many of his disciples drew back" (6:66). In the face of these desertions, Jesus does not compromise and does not mince words; indeed, he demands that a precise choice be made: either to stay with him or leave him, and he says to the Twelve, "Will you also go away?" (6:67).

At this point, Peter makes his confession of faith on behalf of the other apostles: "Lord, to whom shall we go? You have the words of eternal life" (John 6:68). He does not say, "Where shall we go?" but "To whom shall we go?" The underlying problem is not about leaving and abandoning the work undertaken but *to whom* to go.

From Peter's question we understand that fidelity to God is a question of fidelity to a person, to whom we bind ourselves to walk together on the same road. And this person is Jesus. All that we have in the world does not satisfy our infinite hunger. We need Jesus, to be with him, to be nourished at his table, on his words of eternal life! Believing in Jesus means making him the center, the meaning of our life. Christ is not an optional element: he is the "Living Bread," the essential nourishment. Binding oneself to him, in a true relationship of faith and love, does not mean being tied down but being profoundly free, always on the journey. Each one of us can ask himself or herself: who is Jesus for me? Is he a name, an idea, simply an historical figure? Or is he truly that person who loves me and gave his life for me and walks with me? Who is Jesus for you? Are you with Jesus? Do you try to comprehend him in his word? Do you read the Gospel, each day a passage from the Gospel, to learn to know Jesus? Do you carry a small Gospel in your pocket, handbag, to read it, in whatever place? Because the more we are with him, the more the desire to be with him grows. Now I ask you, please, let us have a moment of silence and let each one of us, silently, in our hearts, ask ourselves the question "Who is Jesus for me?" Silently, each one, answer in your heart.

May the Virgin Mary help us to always "go" to Jesus to experience the freedom he offers us, allowing it to cleanse our choices from worldly incrustations and fears.

—ANGELUS ADDRESS, ST. PETER'S SQUARE, AUGUST 23, 2015

32. LET US COME TO THE LIGHT!
JOHN 9:1-41

Today's Gospel sets before us the story of the man born blind, to whom Jesus gives sight. The lengthy account opens with a blind man who begins to see, and it closes—and this is curious—with the alleged seers who remain blind in soul. The miracle is narrated by John in just two verses, because the Evangelist does not want to draw attention to the miracle itself but rather to what follows, to the discussions it arouses, and also to the gossip. So many times a good work, a work of charity, arouses gossip and discussion, because there are some who do not want to see the truth.

The Evangelist John wants to draw attention to something that also occurs in our own day when a good work is performed. The blind man who is healed is first interrogated by the astonished crowd—they saw the miracle and they interrogated him—and then by the doctors of the law, who also interrogate his parents. In the end, the blind man who was healed attains to faith, and this is the greatest grace that Jesus grants him: not only to see, but also to know him, to see in him "the light of the world" (John 9:5).

While the blind man gradually draws near to the light, the doctors of the law, on the contrary, sink deeper and deeper into their inner blindness. Locked in their presumption, they believe that they already have the light; therefore, they do not open themselves to the truth of Jesus. They do everything to deny the evidence. They cast doubt on the identity of the man who was healed; they then deny God's action in the healing, taking as an excuse that God does not work on the Sabbath; they even doubt that the man was born blind. Their closure to the light becomes aggressive and leads to the expulsion from the Temple of the man who was healed.

The blind man's journey, on the contrary, is a journey in stages that begins with the knowledge of Jesus' name. He does not know anything else about him; in fact, he says, "The man called Jesus made clay and anointed my eyes" (John 9:11). Following the pressing questions of the lawyers, he first considers him a prophet (9:17) and then a man who is close to God (9:31).

Once he has been banished from the Temple, expelled from society, Jesus finds him again and "opens his eyes" for the second time, by revealing his own identity to him: "I am the Messiah," he tells him. At this point, the man who had been blind exclaims, "Lord, I believe!" (John 9:38), and he prostrates himself before Jesus. This is a passage of the Gospel that makes evident the drama of the inner blindness of so many people; also our own, for sometimes we have moments of inner blindness.

Our lives are sometimes similar to that of the blind man who opened himself to the light, who opened himself to God, who opened himself to his grace. Sometimes, unfortunately, they are similar to that of the doctors of the law: from the height of our pride we judge others, and even the Lord!

Today we are invited to open ourselves to the light of Christ in order to bear fruit in our lives, to eliminate unchristian behaviors; we are all Christians, but we all, everyone, sometimes have unchristian behaviors, behaviors that are sins. We must repent of this and eliminate these behaviors in order to journey well along the way of holiness, which has its origin in baptism. We, too, have been "enlightened" by Christ in baptism so that, as St. Paul reminds us, we may act as "children of light" (Ephesians 5:8), with humility, patience, and mercy. These doctors of the law had neither humility, nor patience, nor mercy!

I suggest that today, when you return home, you take the Gospel of John and read this passage from chapter nine. It will do you good, because you will thus see this road from blindness to light and the other evil road that leads to deeper blindness.

Let us ask ourselves about the state of our own heart. Do I have an open heart or a closed heart? Is it opened or closed to God? Open or closed to my neighbor? We are always closed to some degree, which comes from original sin, from mistakes, from errors. We need not be afraid! Let us open ourselves to the light of the Lord; he awaits us always in order to enable us to see better, to give us more light, to forgive us. Let us not forget this!

—Angelus Address, St. Peter's Square, March 30, 2014

33. COME OUT OF YOUR TOMB!
JOHN 11:1-45

Today's three readings speak to us about the resurrection; they speak to us about life. This beautiful promise from the Lord, "Behold, I will open your graves, and raise you from your graves" (Ezekiel 37:12), is the promise of the Lord who possesses life and has the power to give life: that those who are dead might regain life. The second reading tells us that we are under the Holy Spirit and that Christ in us, his Spirit, will raise us. And in the third reading of the Gospel, we saw how Jesus gave life to Lazarus. Lazarus, who was dead, has returned to life.

I would simply like to say something very briefly. We all have within us some areas, some parts of our heart, that are not alive, that are a little dead; and some of us have many dead places in our hearts, a true spiritual necrosis! And when we are in this situation, we know it; we want to get out but we can't. Only the power of Jesus, the power of Jesus, can help us come out of these atrophied zones of the heart, these tombs of sin, which we all have.

We are all sinners! But if we become very attached to these tombs and guard them within us and do not will that our whole heart rise again to life, we become corrupted and our soul begins to give off, as Martha says, an "odor" (John 11:39)—the stench of a person who is attached to sin. And Lent is something to do with this, because all of us, who are sinners, do not end up attached to sin but [so] that we can hear what Jesus said to

Lazarus: "He cried out with a loud voice, 'Lazarus, come out'" (cf. 11:43).

Today I invite you to think for a moment, in silence, here: where is my interior necrosis? Where is the dead part of my soul? Where is my tomb? Think, for a short moment, all of you in silence. Let us think: what part of the heart can be corrupted because of my attachment to sin, one sin or another? And [I invite you] to remove the stone, to take away the stone of shame and allow the Lord to say to us, as he said to Lazarus, "Come out!" That all our soul might be healed, might be raised by the love of Jesus, by the power of Jesus. He is capable of forgiving us.

We all need it! All of us. We are all sinners, but we must be careful not to become corrupt! Sinners we may be, but he forgives us. Let us hear that voice of Jesus, who, by the power of God, says to us, "Come out! Leave that tomb you have within you. Come out. I give you life, I give you happiness, I bless you, I want you for myself."

May the Lord today, on this Sunday, which speaks so much about the resurrection, give us all the grace to rise from our sins, to come out of our tombs; with the voice of Jesus, calling us to go out, to go to him.

—HOMILY, PASTORAL VISIT TO THE ROMAN PARISH OF
SAN GREGORIO MAGNO, APRIL 6, 2014

34. "WE WISH TO SEE JESUS"

JOHN 12:20-33

John the Evangelist draws our attention with a curious detail: some "Greeks," of the Jewish religion, who have come to Jerusalem for the feast of Passover, turn to Philip and say to him, "We wish to see Jesus" (John 12:21). There are many people in the holy city, where Jesus has come for the last time; there are many people. There are the little ones and the simple ones, who have warmly welcomed the prophet of Nazareth, recognizing him as the messenger of the Lord. There are the high priests and the leaders of the people, who want to eliminate him because they consider him a heretic and dangerous. There are also people, like those "Greeks," who are curious to see him and to know more about his person and about the works he has performed, the last of which—the resurrection of Lazarus—has caused quite a stir.

"We wish to see Jesus": these words, like so many others in the Gospels, go beyond this particular episode and express something *universal*. They reveal *a desire that passes through the ages and cultures*, a desire present in the heart of so many people who have heard of Christ, but have not yet *encountered* him. "I wish to see Jesus"; thus, he feels the heart of these people.

Responding indirectly, in a prophetic way, to that request to be able to see him, Jesus pronounces a prophecy that reveals his identity and shows the path to know him truly: "The hour has come for the Son of Man to be glorified" (John 12:23). It is *the hour of the cross!* It is the time for the defeat of Satan, prince of evil, and of the definitive triumph of the merciful love of God.

Christ declares that he will be "lifted up from the earth" (John 12:32), an expression with a twofold meaning: "lifted" because he is crucified, and "lifted" because he is exalted by the Father in the resurrection, to draw everyone to him and to reconcile mankind with God and among themselves. The hour of the cross, the darkest in history, is also the source of salvation for those who believe in him.

Continuing in his prophecy of the imminent Passover, Jesus uses a simple and suggestive image, that of the "'grain of wheat' that, once fallen into the earth, dies in order to bear fruit" (cf. John 12:24). In this image we find another aspect of the cross of Christ: that of *fruitfulness*. The death of Jesus, in fact, is an inexhaustible source of new life, because it carries within itself the regenerative strength of God's love. Immersed in this love through baptism, Christians can become "grains of wheat" and bear much fruit if they, like Jesus, "lose their life" out of love for God and [their] brothers and sisters (cf. 12:25).

For this reason, to those who, today too, "wish to see Jesus," to those who are searching for the face of God, to those who received catechesis when they were little and then developed it no further and perhaps have lost their faith, to so many who have not yet encountered Jesus personally . . . to all these people we can offer three things: *the Gospel, the crucifix,* and *the witness* of our faith: poor but sincere.

The Gospel: there we can encounter Jesus, listen to him, know him. The crucifix: the sign of the love of Jesus who gave himself

101

for us. And then a faith that is expressed in simple gestures of fraternal charity. But mainly in the coherence of life, between what we say and what we do. Coherence between our faith and our life, between our words and our actions: Gospel, crucifix, witness.

May Our Lady help us to bring these three things forth.

—ANGELUS ADDRESS, ST. PETER'S SQUARE, MARCH 22, 2015

35. "COME TO ME!"
MATTHEW 11:25-30

In this Sunday's Gospel, we find Jesus' invitation: "Come to me, all who labor and are heavy laden, and I will give you rest" (Matthew 11:28). When Jesus says this, he has before him the people he meets every day on the streets of Galilee: very many simple people, the poor, the sick, sinners, those who are marginalized . . . These people always followed him to hear his word—a word that gave hope! Jesus' words always give hope!—and even just to touch a hem of his garment.

Jesus himself sought out these tired, worn-out crowds like sheep without a shepherd (cf. Matthew 9:35-36), and he sought them out to proclaim to them the kingdom of God and to heal many of them in body and spirit. Now he calls them all to himself: "Come to me," and he promises them relief and rest.

This invitation of Jesus reaches to our day, and extends to the many brothers and sisters oppressed by life's precarious conditions, by existential and difficult situations, and at times lacking valid points of reference. In the poorest countries, but also on the outskirts of the richest countries, there are so many weary people, worn out under the unbearable weight of neglect and indifference. Indifference: human indifference causes the needy so much pain! And worse, the indifference of Christians!

On the fringes of society, so many men and women are tried by indigence but also by dissatisfaction with life and by frustration. So many are forced to emigrate from their homeland, risking their lives. Many more, every day, carry the weight of an economic system that exploits human beings, imposing on them an unbearable "yoke," which the few privileged do not want to bear. To each of these children of the Father in heaven, Jesus repeats, "Come to me, all of you." But he also says it to those who have everything but whose hearts are empty and without God. Even to them, Jesus addresses this invitation: "Come to me." Jesus' invitation is for everyone, but especially for those who suffer the most.

Jesus promises to give rest to everyone, but he also gives us an invitation, which is like a commandment: "Take my yoke upon you, and learn from me; for I am gentle and lowly in heart" (Matthew 11:29). The "yoke" of the Lord consists in taking on the burden of others with fraternal love. Once Christ's comfort and rest is received, we are called in turn to become rest and comfort for our brothers and sisters, with a docile and humble attitude, in imitation of the Teacher. Docility and humility of heart help us not only to take on the burden of others, but also to keep our personal views, our judgments, our criticism, or our indifference from weighing on them.

Let us invoke Mary Most Holy, who welcomes under her mantle all the tired and worn-out people, so that through an enlightened faith, witnessed in life, we can offer relief for so many in need of help, of tenderness, of hope.

—ANGELUS ADDRESS, ST. PETER'S SQUARE, JULY 6, 2014

36. THE PRIMACY OF THE HEART
Mark 7:1-8, 14-15, 21-23

The Gospel for this Sunday concerns a dispute between Jesus and several Pharisees and scribes. The discussion is about the value of the "tradition of the elders" (Mark 7:3), which Jesus, quoting the prophet Isaiah, defines as the "precepts of men" which must never take precedence over the "commandment of God" (7:7, 8). The ancient rules in question consisted not only in the precepts God revealed to Moses, but in a series of norms that the Mosaic law indicated. The interlocutors observed these norms in an extremely scrupulous manner and presented them as the expression of authentic religiosity. Therefore, they rebuked Jesus and his disciples for transgressing them, specifically the norms regarding the external purification of the body (cf. 7:5). Jesus' response has the force of a prophetic pronouncement: "You leave the commandment of God," he says, "and hold fast the tradition of men" (7:8). These are words which fill us with admiration for our Teacher: we sense that in him there is truth and that his wisdom frees us from prejudice.

Pay heed! With these words, Jesus wants to caution us too today against the belief that outward observance of the law is enough to make us good Christians. Dangerous as it was then for the Pharisees, so too is it for us to consider ourselves acceptable or, even worse, better than others simply for observing the rules and customs even though we do not love our neighbor, we are hard of heart, we are arrogant and proud. Literal observance of the precepts is a fruitless exercise which does not change the heart and turn into practical behavior: opening oneself to meet God and his word in prayer, seeking justice and peace, taking care of the poor, the weak, the downtrodden. We all know, in our communities, in our parishes, in our neighborhoods, how much harm and scandal are done to the Church by those people who say they are deeply Catholic and often go to church, but who then neglect their family in daily life, speak badly of others, and so on. This is what Jesus condemns because this is a counterwitness to Christianity.

After his exhortation, Jesus focuses attention on a deeper aspect and states, "There is nothing outside a man which by going into him can defile him; but the things which come out of a man are what defile him" (Mark 7:15). In this way, he emphasizes the primacy of interiority, that is, the primacy of the "heart": it is not the external things that make us holy or unholy, but the heart which expresses our intentions, our choices, and the will to do all for the love of God. External behavior is the result of what we decide in the heart, and not the contrary: with a change in external behavior but not a change of heart, we are not true Christians. The boundary between good and evil does not pass outside of us but rather within us.

We could ask ourselves: where is my heart? Jesus said, "Where your treasure is, there will your heart be also" [Matthew 6:21]. What is my treasure? Is it Jesus, is it his teaching? If so, then the heart is good. Or is my treasure something else? Thus, it is a heart which needs purification and conversion. Without a purified heart, one cannot have truly clean hands and lips which speak sincere words of love—it is all duplicitous, a double life.

Lips which speak words of mercy, of forgiveness: only a sincere and purified heart can do this.

Let us ask the Lord, through the intercession of the Blessed Virgin, to give us a pure heart, free of all hypocrisy. This is the word that Jesus uses for the Pharisees: "hypocrites," because they say one thing and do another. A heart free from all hypocrisy; thus, we will be able to live according to the spirit of the law and accomplish its aim, which is love.

—ANGELUS ADDRESS, ST. PETER'S SQUARE, AUGUST 30, 2015

37. "BE OPENED!"
MARK 7:31-37

The Gospel today recounts Jesus' healing of a man who was deaf and had a speech impediment, an incredible event that shows how Jesus reestablishes the full communication of man with God and with other people. The miracle is set in the region of the Decapolis, that is, in a completely pagan territory; thus, this deaf man who is brought before Jesus becomes the symbol of an unbeliever who completes a journey to faith. In effect, his deafness expresses the inability to hear and to understand, not just the words of man, but also the word of God. And St. Paul reminds us that "faith comes from what is heard" (Romans 10:17).

The first thing that Jesus does is take this man *far from the crowd*: he doesn't want to publicize this deed he intends to carry out, but he also doesn't want his word to be lost in the din of voices and the chatter of those around. The word of God that Christ brings us needs silence to be welcomed as the word that heals, that reconciles and reestablishes communication.

Then we are told about two gestures Jesus makes. He *touches the ears and the tongue* of the deaf man. To reestablish a relationship with this man whose communication is "impeded," he first seeks to reestablish contact. But the miracle is a gift that comes from on high, which Jesus implores from the Father. That's why he *raises his eyes to the heavens and orders, "Be opened."* And the ears of the deaf man are opened, the knot of his tongue is untied, and he begins to speak correctly (cf. Mark 7:35).

The lesson we can take from this episode is that God is not closed in on himself, but instead, he *opens himself and places himself in communication* with humanity. In his immense mercy, he overcomes the abyss of the infinite difference between him and us and comes to meet us. To bring about this communication with man, God becomes man. It is not enough for him to speak to us through the law and the prophets, but instead, he makes himself present in the person of his Son, the Word made flesh. Jesus is the great "bridge-builder" who builds in himself the great bridge of full communion with the Father.

But this Gospel speaks to us also about ourselves: often we are drawn up and closed in on ourselves, and we create many inaccessible and inhospitable islands. Even the most basic human relationships can sometimes create realities incapable of reciprocal openness: the couple closed in, the family closed in, the group closed in, the parish closed in, the country closed in. And this is not from God! This is from us. This is our sin.

However, at the beginning of our Christian life, at baptism, it is precisely this gesture and word of Jesus that are present: "*Ephphatha!*" "Be opened!" And behold the miracle has been worked. We are healed of the deafness of selfishness and the impediment of being closed in on ourselves, and of sin, and we have been inserted into the great family of the Church. We can hear God who speaks to us and communicates his word to those who have never before heard it, or to the one who has forgotten it and buried it in the thorns of the anxieties and the traps of the world.

Let us ask the Virgin Mary, a woman of listening and of joyful testimony, that she sustain us in the commitment to profess our faith and to communicate the wonders of the Lord to those we find along our way.

—Angelus Address, St. Peter's Square, September 6, 2015

38. THE PARABLE OF THE SEED
MATTHEW 13:1-23

This Sunday's Gospel shows us Jesus preaching on the shore of the Lake of Galilee, and because a large crowd surrounds him, he climbs into a boat, goes a little way from the shore, and preaches from there. When he speaks to the people, Jesus uses many parables: in language understandable to everyone, with images from nature and from everyday situations.

The first story he tells is an introduction to all the parables: that of the sower, who sows his seed unsparingly on every type of soil. And the real protagonist of this parable is actually the seed, which produces more or less according to the type of soil upon which it falls. The first three areas are unproductive: along the path the seed is eaten by birds; on rocky ground the sprouts are scorched and wither away because they have no roots; among the briars the seed is choked by thorns. The fourth piece of ground is good soil, and only there does the seed take root and bear fruit.

In this case, Jesus does not limit himself to presenting this parable; he also explains it to his disciples. The seed fallen on the path stands for those who hear the message of the kingdom of God but do not understand it; thus, the evil one comes and snatches it away. Indeed, the evil one does not want the seed of the gospel to sprout in the heart of man. This is the first analogy.

The second is that of the seed fallen among the stones: this represents the people who hear the word of God and understand it immediately but superficially, because they have no roots and they are unsettled. When trials and tribulations arise, these people give up immediately.

The third case is that of the seed fallen among the briars: Jesus explains that this refers to the people who hear the word, but they, because of the cares of the world and the seduction of riches, are choked. Finally, the seed fallen on fertile soil represents those who hear the word, accept it, cherish it, and understand it, and they bear fruit. The perfect model of this good soil is the Virgin Mary.

This parable speaks to each of us today, as it spoke to those who listened to Jesus two thousand years ago. It reminds us that we are the soil where the Lord tirelessly sows the seed of his word and of his love. How do we receive it? And we can ask ourselves: how is our heart? Which soil does it resemble: that of the path, the rocks, the thorns? It's up to us to become good soil with neither thorns nor stones, but tilled and cultivated with care, so it may bear good fruit for us and for our brothers and sisters.

And it will do us good not to forget that we, too, are sowers. God sows good seed, and here too we can also ask ourselves: which type of seed comes out of our heart and our mouth? Our words can do much good and also much harm; they can heal and they can wound; they can encourage and they can dishearten. Remember: what counts is not what goes in but what comes out of the mouth and of the heart.

Our Lady teaches us, by her example, to understand the word, cherish it, and make it bear fruit in us and in others.

—ANGELUS ADDRESS, ST. PETER'S SQUARE, JULY 13, 2014

39. GOD IS PATIENT
MATTHEW 13:24-30, 36-43

These Sundays the liturgy proposes several Gospel parables, that is, short stories which Jesus used to announce the kingdom of heaven to the crowds. Among those in today's Gospel, there is a rather complex one which Jesus explained to the disciples: it is that of *the good grain and the weed*, which deals with *the problem of evil* in the world and calls attention to *God's patience* (cf. Matthew 13:24-30, 36-43).

The story takes place in a field where the owner sows grain, but during the night his enemy comes and sows weed, a term which in Hebrew derives from the same root as the name "Satan" and which alludes to the concept of division. We all know that the demon is a "sower of weed," one who always seeks to sow division between individuals, families, nations, and peoples. The servants wanted to uproot the weed immediately, but the field owner stopped them, explaining that "in gathering the weeds you root up the wheat along with them" (Matthew 13:29). Because we all know that a weed, when it grows, looks very much like good grain, and there is the risk of confusing them.

The teaching of the parable is twofold. First of all, it tells that the evil in the world *comes not from God but from his enemy, the evil one*. It is curious that the evil one goes at night to sow weed, in the dark, in confusion; he goes where there is no light to sow weed. This enemy is astute: he sows evil in the middle of good; thus, it is impossible for us men to distinctly separate them; but God, in the end, will be able to do so.

And here we arrive at the second theme: the juxtaposition of the impatience of the servants and the *patient waiting* of the field owner, who represents God. At times we are in a great hurry to judge, to categorize, to put the good here, the bad there ... But remember the prayer of that self-righteous man: "God, I thank you that I am good, that I am not like other men, malicious" (cf. Luke 18:11-12).

God, however, knows how to wait. With patience and mercy he gazes into the "field" of life of every person; he sees much better than we do the filth and the evil, but he also sees the seeds of good and waits with trust for them to grow. God is patient; he knows how to wait. This is so beautiful: our God is a patient father who always waits for us and waits with his heart in hand to welcome us, to forgive us. He always forgives us if we go to him.

The field owner's attitude is that of hope grounded in the certainty that evil does not have the first or the last word. And it is thanks to this *patient hope* of God that the same weed, which is the malicious heart with so many sins, in the end can become good grain. But be careful: evangelical patience is not indifference to evil; one must not confuse good and evil! In facing weeds in the world, the Lord's disciple is called to imitate the patience of God, to nourish hope with the support of indestructible trust in the final victory of good, that is, of God.

In the end, in fact, evil will be removed and eliminated: at the time of harvest, that is, of judgment, the harvesters will follow the orders of the field owner, separating the weed to burn it (cf. Matthew 13:30). On the day of the final harvest, *the judge will be Jesus*, he who has sown good grain in the world and who himself became the "*grain of wheat*," who died and rose.

In the end, we will all be judged by the same measure with which we have judged: *the mercy we have shown to others will also be shown to us*. Let us ask Our Lady, our Mother, to help us to grow in patience, in hope, and in mercy with all [our[brothers and sisters.

—ANGELUS ADDRESS, ST. PETER'S SQUARE, JULY 20, 2014

40. DISCOVERING THE KINGDOM OF GOD
MATTHEW 13:44-52

The brief similes proposed in today's liturgy conclude the chapter of the Gospel of Matthew dedicated to the parables of the kingdom of God. Among these are two small masterpieces: the parables of the treasure hidden in the field and of the pearl of great value. They tell us that the discovery of the kingdom of God can happen *suddenly* like the farmer who, plowing, finds an unexpected treasure; or *after a long search*, like the pearl merchant who eventually finds the most precious pearl, so long dreamt of.

Yet in each case, the point is that the treasure and the pearl are worth more than all other possessions, and therefore, when the farmer and the merchant discover them, they give up everything else in order to obtain them. They do not need to rationalize or think about it or reflect: they immediately perceive the incomparable value of what they've found, and they are prepared to lose everything in order to have it.

This is how it is with the kingdom of God: those who find it have no doubts; they sense that this is what they have been seeking and waiting for, and this is what fulfills their most authentic aspirations. And it really is like this: those who know Jesus, encounter him personally, are *captivated, attracted* by so much goodness, so much truth, so much beauty, and all with great humility and simplicity. To seek Jesus, to find Jesus: this is the great treasure!

Many people, many saints, reading the Gospel with an open heart, have been so struck by Jesus that they converted to him. Let us think of St. Francis of Assisi: he was already a Christian, though a "rosewater" Christian. When he read the Gospel, in that decisive moment of his youth, he encountered Jesus and discovered the kingdom of God; with this, all his dreams of worldly glory vanished. The Gospel allows you to know the real Jesus; it lets you know the living Jesus; it speaks to your heart and changes your life. And then, yes, you leave it all. You can effectively change lifestyles or continue to do what you did before, but *you* are someone else, you are reborn: you have found what gives meaning, what gives flavor, what gives light to all things, even to toil, even to suffering, and even to death.

Read the Gospel. Read the Gospel. We have spoken about it, do you remember? To read a passage of the Gospel every day; and to carry a little Gospel with us, in our pocket, in a purse, in some way to keep it at hand. And there, reading a passage, we will find Jesus. Everything takes on meaning when you find your treasure there, in the Gospel. Jesus calls it "the kingdom of God," that is to say, God who reigns in your life, in our life; God who is love, peace, and joy in every man and in all men. This is what God wants, and it is why Jesus gave himself up to death on the cross, to free us from the power of darkness and to move us to the kingdom of life, of beauty, of goodness, and of joy. To read the Gospel is to find Jesus and to have this Christian joy, which is a gift of the Holy Spirit.

Dear brothers and sisters, the joy of finding the treasure of the kingdom of God shines through; it's visible. The Christian cannot keep his faith hidden because it shines through in every word, in every deed, even the most simple and mundane: the love that God has given through Jesus shines through. Let us pray, through the intercession of the Virgin Mary, that his kingdom of love, justice, and peace may reign in us and in the whole world.

—ANGELUS ADDRESS, ST. PETER'S SQUARE, JULY 27, 2014

41. COMPASSION, SHARING, EUCHARIST
MATTHEW 14:13-21

This Sunday the Gospel presents to us the miracle of the multiplication of loaves and fish. Jesus performed it along the Lake of Galilee, in a deserted place where he had withdrawn with his disciples after learning of the death of John the Baptist. But many people followed them and joined them there; and upon seeing them, Jesus felt compassion and healed their sick until the evening. And seeing the late hour, the disciples became concerned and suggested that Jesus send the crowd away so they could go into the villages and buy food to eat. But Jesus calmly replied, "You give them something to eat" (Matthew 14:16); and he asked them to bring five loaves and two fish, blessed them, began to break them and give them to the disciples, who distributed them to the people. They all ate and were satisfied, and there were even leftovers!

We can understand three messages from this event. The first is *compassion*. In facing the crowd who follows him and—so to speak—"won't leave him alone," Jesus does not react with irritation; he does not say, "These people are bothering me." No, no. He reacts with a feeling of compassion, because he knows they are not seeking him out of curiosity but out of need. But attention: compassion—which Jesus feels—is not simply feeling pity; it's more! It means to *suffer with*; in other words, to empathize with the suffering of another, to the point of taking it upon oneself.

Jesus is like this: he suffers together with us, he suffers with us, he suffers for us. And the sign of this compassion is the healing of countless people he performed. Jesus teaches us to place the needs of the poor before our own. Our needs, even if legitimate, are not as urgent as those of the poor, who lack the basic necessities of life. We often speak of the poor. But when we speak of the poor, do we sense that this man or that woman or those children lack the bare necessities of life? That they have no food, they have no clothing, they cannot afford medicine? Also that the children do not have the means to attend school? Whereas our needs, although legitimate, are not as urgent as those of the poor who lack life's basic necessities.

The second message is *sharing*. The first is compassion, which Jesus felt, and the second is sharing. It's helpful to compare the reaction of the disciples with regard to the tired and hungry people with that of Jesus. They are different. The disciples think it would be better to send them away so they can go and buy food. Jesus instead says, "You give them something to eat."

Two different reactions, which reflect two contrasting outlooks: the disciples reason with worldly logic, by which each person must think of himself; they reason as if to say, "Sort it out for yourselves." Jesus reasons with God's logic, which is that of sharing. How many times we turn away so as not to see our brothers in need! And this looking away is a polite way to say, with white gloves, "Sort it out for yourselves."

And this is not Jesus' way: this is selfishness. Had he sent away the crowds, many people would have been left with nothing to eat. Instead, those few loaves and fish, shared and blessed by God, were enough for everyone. And pay heed! It isn't magic, it's a "sign": a sign that calls for faith in God, provident Father, who does not let us go without "our daily bread," if we know how to share it as brothers.

Compassion, sharing. And the third message: the miracle of the loaves foreshadows the *Eucharist*. It is seen in the gesture of Jesus who, before breaking and distributing the loaves, "blessed" them (Matthew 14:19). It is the same gesture that Jesus was to make at the Last Supper, when he established the perpetual memorial of his redeeming sacrifice.

In the Eucharist, Jesus does not give just any bread, but *the* bread of eternal life; he gives himself, offering himself to the Father out of love for us. But we must go to the Eucharist with those sentiments of Jesus, which are compassion and the will to share. One who goes to the Eucharist without having compassion for the needy and without sharing is not at ease with Jesus.

Compassion, sharing, Eucharist. This is the path that Jesus points out to us in this Gospel. A path which brings us to face the needs of this world with fraternity, but which leads us beyond this world, because it comes from God the Father and returns to him. May the Virgin Mary, Mother of Divine Providence, accompany us on this journey.

—ANGELUS ADDRESS, ST. PETER'S SQUARE, AUGUST 3, 2014

42. SAFE IN THE BOAT
MATTHEW 14:22-33

In today's Gospel, we are presented with the account of Jesus walking on the water of the lake. After the multiplication of loaves and fish, he asks the disciples to get into the boat and go before him to the other side of the lake while he dismisses the crowds. He then goes up into the hills by himself to pray until late at night. Meanwhile, a strong storm blows up on the lake, and right in the middle of the storm, Jesus reaches the disciples' boat, walking upon the water of the lake. When they see him, the disciples are terrified, but he calms them: "Take heart, it is I; have no fear!" (Matthew 14:27). Peter, with his usual passion, practically puts him to the test: "Lord, if it is you, bid me come to you on the water"; and Jesus answers, "Come!" (14:28, 29). Peter gets out of the boat and walks on the water, but a strong wind hits him and he begins to sink. And so he yells, "Lord, save me!" (14:30), and Jesus reaches out his hand and catches him.

This story is a beautiful icon of the faith of the apostle Peter. In the voice of Jesus who tells him, "Come!" he recognizes the echo of the first encounter on the shore of that very lake, and right away, once again, he leaves the boat and goes toward the Teacher. And he walks on the waters! The faithful and ready response to the Lord's call always enables one to achieve extraordinary things.

But Jesus himself told us that we are capable of performing miracles with our faith, faith in him, faith in his word, faith in his voice. Peter, however, begins to sink the moment he looks away from Jesus, and he allows himself to be overwhelmed by the hardships around him. But the Lord is always there, and when Peter calls him, Jesus saves him from danger. Peter's character, with his passion and his weaknesses, can describe our faith: ever fragile and impoverished, anxious yet victorious, Christian faith walks to meet the risen Lord amid the world's storms and dangers.

And the final scene is also very important. "And when they got into the boat, the wind ceased. And those in the boat worshiped him, saying, 'Truly you are the Son of God!'" (Matthew 14:32-33). All the disciples are on the boat, united in the experience of weakness, of doubt, of fear, and of "little faith." But when Jesus climbs into that boat again, the weather suddenly changes: they all feel united in their faith in him. All the little and frightened ones become great at the moment in which they fall on their knees and recognize the Son of God in their teacher. How many times the same thing happens to us! Without Jesus, far from Jesus, we feel frightened and inadequate to the point of thinking we cannot succeed. Faith is lacking! But Jesus is always with us, hidden perhaps, but present and ready to support us.

This is an effective image of the Church: a boat which must brave the storms and sometimes seems on the point of capsizing. What saves her is not the skill and courage of her crew members but faith, which allows her to walk, even in the dark, amid hardships. Faith gives us the certainty of Jesus' presence always beside us, of his hand which grasps us to pull us back from danger. We are all on this boat, and we feel secure here despite our limitations and our weaknesses. We are safe especially when we are ready to kneel and worship Jesus, the only Lord of our life. This is what our Mother, Our Lady, always reminds us. We turn to her trustingly.

—Angelus Address, St. Peter's Square, August 10, 2014

43. "WHO DO YOU SAY THAT I AM?"
MATTHEW 16:13-20

This Sunday's Gospel reading is a well-known passage, central to Matthew's account, in which Simon, on behalf of the Twelve, professes his faith in Jesus as "the Christ, the Son of the living God"; and Jesus calls Simon "blessed" for this faith, recognizing in him a special gift of the Father, and tells him, "You are Peter, and on this rock I will build my church" [16:16, 18].

Let us pause on this very point, on the fact that Jesus gives Simon this name, "Peter," which in Jesus' language is pronounced "*Kefa,*" a word which means "rock." In the Bible this term "rock" refers to God. Jesus gives it to Simon, not because of his character or for his merits as a human, but for his *genuine and steadfast faith*, which comes to him from above.

Jesus feels great joy in his heart because in Simon he recognizes the hand of the Father, the work of the Holy Spirit. He recognizes that God the Father has given Simon "steadfast" faith on which he, Jesus, can build his Church, meaning his community, that is, all of us. Jesus intends to give life to "his" Church, a people founded no longer on heritage but on *faith*, which means on the relationship with him, a relationship of love and trust. The Church is built on our relationship with Jesus. And to begin his Church, Jesus needs to find solid faith, "steadfast" faith in his disciples. And it is this that he must verify at this point of the journey.

The Lord has in mind a picture of the structure, an image of the community like a building. This is why, when he hears Simon's candid profession of faith, he calls him a "rock" and declares his intention to build his Church upon this faith.

Brothers and sisters, what happened in a unique way in St. Peter also happens in every Christian who develops a sincere faith in Jesus the Christ, the Son of the living God. Today's Gospel passage also asks each of us: is your faith good? Each one must answer in his or her heart. Is my faith good? How does the Lord find our hearts? A heart that is firm as a rock, or a heart like sand, that is doubtful, diffident, disbelieving? It will do us good to think about this throughout the day today.

If the Lord finds in our heart, I don't say a perfect, but sincere, genuine faith, then he also sees in us living stones with which to build his community. This community's foundation stone is Christ, the unique cornerstone. On his side, Peter is the rock, the visible foundation of the Church's unity; but every baptized person is called to offer Jesus his or her lowly but sincere faith, so that he may continue to build his Church, today, in every part of the world.

Even today, so many people think Jesus may be a great prophet, knowledgeable teacher, a model of justice . . . And even today, Jesus asks his disciples, that is, all of us, "Who do you say that I am?" What do we answer? Let us think about this.

But above all, let us pray to God the Father, through the intercession of the Virgin Mary; let us pray that he grant us the grace to respond, with a sincere heart: "You are the Christ, the Son of the living God." This is a confession of faith, this is really "the Creed." Let us repeat it together three times: "You are the Christ, the Son of the living God."

—ANGELUS ADDRESS, ST. PETER'S SQUARE, AUGUST 24, 2014

44. CONFORMED TO CHRIST
MATTHEW 16:21-27

Sunday's reading from the Gospel according to Matthew brings us to the critical point at which Jesus, after having ascertained that Peter and the other eleven believed in him as the Messiah and Son of God, "began to show his disciples that he must go to Jerusalem and suffer many things . . . , and be killed, and on the third day be raised" (Matthew 16:21). It is a critical moment at which the contrast between Jesus' way of thinking and that of the disciples emerges.

Peter actually feels duty bound to admonish the Master because the Messiah could not come to such an ignominious end. Then Jesus, in turn, severely rebukes Peter and puts him in his place, because he is "not on the side of God, but of men" (Matthew 16:23), unintentionally playing the part of Satan, the tempter. The apostle Paul also stresses this point when he writes to the Christians in Rome, telling them, "Do not be conformed to this world but be transformed by the renewal of your mind, that you may prove what is the will of God, what is good and acceptable and perfect" (Romans 12:2).

Indeed, we Christians live in the world, fully integrated into the social and cultural reality of our time, and rightly so; but this brings with it the risk that we might become "worldly," that "the salt might lose its taste," as Jesus would say (cf. Matthew 5:13). In other words, the Christian could become "watered down," losing the charge of newness which comes to him from the Lord and from the Holy Spirit. . . . It is sad to find "watered-down"

Christians, who seem like watered-down wine. One cannot tell whether they are Christian or worldly; like watered-down wine, one cannot tell whether it is wine or water! This is sad. It is sad to find Christians who are no longer the salt of the earth, and we know that when salt loses its taste, it is no longer good for anything. Their salt has lost its taste because they have delivered themselves up to the spirit of the world; that is, they have become worldly.

This is why it is necessary to renew oneself by continually drawing sap from the Gospel. And how can one do this in practice? First of all by actually reading and meditating on the Gospel every day so the word of Jesus may always be present in our life. Remember: it will help you to always carry the Gospel with you: a small Gospel, in a pocket, in a bag, and read a passage during the day. But always with the Gospel, because it is carrying the word of Jesus, and being able to read it.

In addition, attending Sunday Mass, where we encounter the Lord in the community, we hear his word and receive the Eucharist, which unites us with him and to one another; and then days of retreat and spiritual exercises are very important for spiritual renewal. Gospel, Eucharist, prayer. Do not forget: Gospel, Eucharist, prayer. Thanks to these gifts of the Lord, we are able to conform not to the world but to Christ, and follow him on his path, the path of "losing one's life" in order to find it (cf. Matthew 16:25). "To lose it" in the sense of giving it, offering it through love and in love—and this leads to sacrifice, also the cross—to receive it liberated from selfishness and from the mortgage of death, newly purified, full of eternity.

May the Virgin Mary always go before us on this journey; let us be guided and accompanied by her.

—Angelus Address, St. Peter's Square, August 31, 2014

45. WE ARE ALL SINNERS
MATTHEW 18:15-20

The Gospel this Sunday . . . presents the theme of brotherly correction within the community of believers: that is, how I must correct another Christian when he does what is not good. Jesus teaches us that, should my Christian brother commit a sin against me, offend me, I must be charitable toward him and, first of all, speak with him personally, explain to him what he said or did that was wrong. What if the brother doesn't listen to me? Jesus proposes a progressive intervention: first, return and speak to him with two or three other people so he may be more aware of his error; if, despite this, he does not accept the admonition, the community must be told; and should he also refuse to listen to the community, he must be made aware of the rift and estrangement that he himself has caused, weakening the communion with his brothers in the faith.

The stages of this plan show the effort that the Lord asks of his community in order to accompany the one who transgresses so that he or she is not lost. It is important above all to prevent any clamor in the news and gossip in the community—this is the first thing; this must be avoided. "Go and tell him his fault, between you and him alone" (Matthew 18:15). The approach is one of sensitivity, prudence, humility, attention toward the one who committed a fault, to avoid wounding or killing the brother with words. Because, you know, words, too, can kill!

When I speak, when I make an unfair criticism, when I "flay" a brother with my tongue, this is killing another person's reputation! Words kill too. Let us pay attention to this. At the same time, the discretion of speaking to him alone is to avoid needlessly humiliating the sinner. It is discussed between the two, no one is aware of it, and then it's over.

This requirement also takes into account the consequent series of interventions calling for the involvement of a few witnesses and then actually of the community. The purpose is to help the person realize what he has done, and that through his fault he has offended not only one, but everyone. But it also helps us to free ourselves from anger or resentment, which only causes harm: that bitterness of heart which brings anger and resentment and which leads us to insult and aggression. It's terrible to see an insult or taunt issue from the mouth of a Christian. It is ugly. Do you understand? Do not insult! To insult is not Christian. Understood? To insult is not Christian.

Actually, before God we are all sinners and in need of forgiveness. All of us. Indeed, Jesus told us not to judge. Fraternal correction is a mark of the love and communion which must reign in the Christian community; it is, rather, a mutual service that we can and must render to one another. To reprove a brother is a service, and it is possible and effective only if each one recognizes oneself to be a sinner and in need of the Lord's forgiveness. The same awareness that enables me to recognize the fault of another, even before that, reminds me that I have likewise made mistakes and I am often wrong.

This is why, at the beginning of Mass, every time, we are called before the Lord to recognize that we are sinners, expressing through words and gestures sincere repentance of the heart.

And we say, "Have mercy on me, Lord. I am a sinner! I confess to almighty God my sins." And we don't say, "Lord, have mercy on this man who is beside me, or this woman, who are sinners." No! "Have mercy on me!" We are all sinners and in need of the Lord's forgiveness. It is the Holy Spirit who speaks to our spirit and makes us recognize our faults in light of the word of Jesus.

And Jesus himself invites us all, saints and sinners, to his table, gathering us from the crossroads, from diverse situations of life (cf. Matthew 22:9-10). And among the conditions in common among those participating in the Eucharistic celebration, two are fundamental in order to go to Mass correctly: we are all sinners, and God grants his mercy to all. These are the two conditions which open wide the doors that we might enter Mass properly. We must always remember this before addressing a brother in brotherly correction.

—Angelus Address, St. Peter's Square, September 7, 2014

46. GOD'S INVITATION IS UNIVERSAL
MATTHEW 22:1-14

In this Sunday's Gospel, Jesus speaks to us about the response given to the invitation from God—who is represented by a king—to participate in a wedding banquet. The invitation has three characteristics: *freely offered, breadth,* and *universality*. Many people were invited, but something surprising happened: none of the intended guests came to take part in the feast, saying they had other things to do; indeed, some were even indifferent, impertinent, even annoyed. God is good to us; he freely offers us his friendship, he freely offers us his joy, his salvation; but so often we do not accept his gifts; we place our practical concerns, our interests, first. And when the Lord is calling to us, it so often seems to annoy us.

Some of the intended guests went so far as to abuse and kill the servants who delivered the invitation. But despite the lack of response from those called, God's plan is never interrupted. In facing the rejection of the first invitees, he is not discouraged, he does not cancel the feast, but makes another invitation, expanding it beyond all reasonable limits, and sends his servants into the town squares and the byways to gather anyone they find. These, however, are ordinary, poor, neglected, and marginalized people, good and bad alike—even bad people are invited—without distinction. And the hall is filled with "the excluded." The gospel, rejected by some, is unexpectedly welcomed in many other hearts.

The goodness of God has no bounds and does not discriminate against anyone. For this reason, the banquet of the Lord's gifts is universal, for everyone. Everyone is given the opportunity to respond to the invitation, to his call; no one has the right to feel privileged or to claim an exclusive right. All of this induces us to break the habit of conveniently placing ourselves at the center, as did the high priests and the Pharisees. One must not do this; we must open ourselves to the peripheries, also acknowledging that, at the margins too, even one who is cast aside and scorned by society is the object of God's generosity. We are all called not to reduce the kingdom of God to the confines of the "little church"—our "tiny little church"—but to enlarge the Church to the dimensions of the kingdom of God. However, there is one condition: wedding attire must be worn, that is, charity toward God and neighbor must be shown.

Let us entrust the tragedies and the hopes of so many of our excluded, weak, outcast, scorned brothers and sisters, as well as of those who are persecuted for reasons of faith, to the intercession of Most Holy Mary.

—Angelus Address, St. Peter's Square, October 12, 2014

47. THE TWOFOLD LAW OF LOVE
MATTHEW 22:34-40

Today's Gospel reading reminds us that the whole of divine law can be summed up in our love for God and neighbor. Matthew the Evangelist recounts that several Pharisees colluded to put Jesus to the test (22:34-35). One of them, a doctor of the law, asked him this question: "Teacher, which is the greatest commandment in the law?" (cf. 22:36). Jesus, quoting the Book of Deuteronomy, answered, "You shall love the Lord your God with all your heart, and with all your soul, and with all your mind. This is the greatest and first commandment" (cf. 12:37-38).

And he could have stopped there. Yet Jesus adds something that was not asked by the doctor of the law. He says, in fact, "And a second is like it, You shall love your neighbor as yourself" (22:39). And in this case too, Jesus does not invent the second commandment, but takes it from the Book of Leviticus. The novelty is in his placing these two commandments together—love for God and love for neighbor—revealing that they are, in fact, inseparable and complementary, two sides of the same coin. You cannot love God without loving your neighbor, and you cannot love your neighbor without loving God. Pope Benedict gave us a beautiful commentary on this topic in his first encyclical, *Deus Caritas Est* (16–18).

In effect, the visible sign a Christian can show in order to witness to his love for God to the world and to others, to his family, is the love he bears for his brothers. The commandment to love

God and neighbor is the first, not because it is at the top of the list of commandments. Jesus does not place it at the pinnacle but at the center, because it is from the heart that everything must go out and to which everything must return and refer.

In the Old Testament, the requirement to be holy, in the image of God who is holy, included the duty to care for the most vulnerable people, such as the stranger, the orphan, and the widow (cf. Exodus 22:20-26). Jesus brings this covenant law to fulfillment; he who unites in himself, in his flesh, divinity and humanity, a single mystery of love.

Now, in the light of this word of Jesus, love is the measure of faith, and faith is the soul of love. We can no longer separate a religious life, a pious life, from service to brothers and sisters, to the real brothers and sisters that we encounter. We can no longer divide prayer, the encounter with God in the sacraments, from listening to the other, closeness to his life, especially to his wounds. Remember this: love is the measure of faith. How much do you love? Each one answer silently. How is your faith? My faith is as I love. And faith is the soul of love.

In the middle of the dense forest of rules and regulations—to the legalisms of past and present—Jesus makes an opening through which one can catch a glimpse of two faces: the face of the Father and the face of the brother. He does not give us two formulas or two precepts: there are no precepts or formulas. He gives us two faces—actually only one real face, that of God reflected in many faces, because in the face of each brother, especially of the smallest, the most fragile, the defenseless and needy, there is God's own image. And we must ask ourselves:

when we meet one of these brothers, are we able to recognize the face of God in him? Are we able to do this?

In this way, Jesus offers to all the fundamental criteria on which to base one's life. But above all, he gave us the Holy Spirit, who allows us to love God and neighbor as he does, with a free and generous heart. With the intercession of Mary, our Mother, let us open ourselves to welcome this gift of love, to walk forever with this twofold law, which really has only one facet: the law of love.

—ANGELUS ADDRESS, ST. PETER'S SQUARE, OCTOBER 26, 2014

48. BEAR FRUIT WITH YOUR TALENTS
MATTHEW 25:14-30

The Gospel this Sunday is the Parable of the Talents. The passage from St. Matthew tells of a man who, before setting off on a journey, calls his servants and entrusts his assets to them in talents, extremely valuable ancient coins. That master entrusts five talents to the first servant, two to the second, and one to the third. During the master's absence, the three servants must earn a profit from this patrimony. The first and second servant each double the initial value of the capital. The third, however, for fear of losing it all, buries the talent he received in a hole. Upon the master's return, the first two receive praise and rewards, while the third, who returned only the coin he had received, is reproached and punished.

The meaning of this is clear. The man in the parable represents Jesus, we are the servants, and the talents are the inheritance that the Lord entrusts to us. What is the inheritance? His word, the Eucharist, faith in the heavenly Father, his forgiveness . . . in other words, so many things, his most precious treasures. This is the inheritance that he entrusts to us, not only to safeguard, but to make fruitful!

While in common usage the term "talent" indicates a pronounced individual quality, for example, talent in music, in sport, and so on, in the parable, talents represent the riches of the Lord, which he entrusts to us so that we make them bear fruit. The hole dug into the soil by the "wicked and slothful servant" (Matthew 25:26) points to the fear of risk, which blocks creativity and the fruitfulness of love, because the fear of the risks of love stops us. Jesus does not ask us to store his grace in a safe!

Jesus does not ask us for this, but he wants us to use it to benefit others. All the goods that we have received are to give to others, and thus they increase, as if he were to tell us, "Here is my mercy, my tenderness, my forgiveness: take them and make ample use of them." And what have we done with them? Whom have we "infected" with our faith? How many people have we encouraged with our hope? How much love have we shared with our neighbor? These are questions that will do us good to ask ourselves. Any environment, even the furthest and most impractical, can become a place where our talents can bear fruit. There are no situations or places precluded from the Christian presence and witness. The witness which Jesus asks of us is not closed but is open; it is in our hands.

This parable urges us not to conceal our faith and our belonging to Christ, not to bury the word of the gospel, but to let it circulate in our life, in our relationships, in concrete situations, as a strength which galvanizes, which purifies, which renews. Similarly, the forgiveness, which the Lord grants us particularly in the Sacrament of Reconciliation: let us not keep it closed within ourselves, but let us allow it to emit its power, which brings down the walls that our egoism has raised, which enables us to take the first step in strained relationships, to resume the dialogue where there is no longer communication. . . . Allow these talents, these gifts, these presents that the Lord has given us, to be, to grow, to bear fruit for others, with our witness.

I think it would be a fine gesture for each of you to pick up the Gospel at home today, the Gospel of St. Matthew, chapter 25, verses 14 to 30, and read this, and meditate a bit: "The talents, the treasures, all that God has given me, all things spiritual, all goodness, the word of God, how do I make this grow in others? Or do I merely store it in a safe?"

Moreover, the Lord does not give the same things to everyone in the same way: he knows us personally and entrusts us with what is right for us; but in everyone, in all, there is something equal: the same, immense trust. God trusts us; God has hope in us! And this is the same for everyone. Let us not disappoint him! Let us not be misled by fear, but let us reciprocate trust with trust!

The Virgin Mary embodied this attitude in the fullest and most beautiful way. She received and welcomed the most sublime gift, Jesus himself, and in turn she offered him to mankind with a generous heart. Let us ask her to help us to be "good and faithful servants" in order to participate "in the joy of our Lord" (cf. Matthew 25:21).

—ANGELUS ADDRESS, ST. PETER'S SQUARE, NOVEMBER 16, 2014

49. THE EUCHARIST: THE SCHOOL OF LOVE
MARK 14:12-16, 22-26

Today in many countries, including Italy, we celebrate the Solemnity of the Most Holy Body and Blood of Christ or, according to the well-known Latin expression, the Solemnity of Corpus Christi.

The Gospel presents the narrative of the institution of the Eucharist, performed by Jesus during the Last Supper in the upper room in Jerusalem. On the eve of his redeeming death on the cross, he fulfilled what had been foretold: "I am the living bread which came down from heaven; if any one eats of this bread, he will live for ever; and the bread which I shall give for the life of the world is my flesh. . . . He who eats my flesh and drinks my blood abides in me, and I in him" (John 6:51, 56). Jesus takes the bread in his hands and says, "Take; this is my body" (Mark 14:22). With this gesture and with these words, he assigns to the bread a function which is no longer simply that of physical nutrition, but that of making his Person present in the midst of the community of believers.

The Last Supper represents the culmination of Christ's entire life. It is not only the anticipation of his sacrifice which will be rendered on the cross, but also the synthesis of a life offered for the salvation of the whole of humanity. Therefore, it is not enough to state that Jesus is present in the Eucharist, but one must see in it the presence of a life given and partake in it. When we take and eat that Bread, we are associated into the life of Jesus, we enter into communion with him, and we commit to

142

achieve communion among ourselves, to transform our life into a gift, especially to the poorest.

Today's feast evokes this message of solidarity and urges us to welcome the intimate invitation to conversion and to service, love, and forgiveness. It urges us to become, with our life, imitators of that which we celebrate in the liturgy. The Christ, who nourishes us under the consecrated species of bread and wine, is the same One who comes to us in the everyday happenings; he is in the poor person who holds out his hand, in the suffering one who begs for help, in the brother or sister who asks for our availability and awaits our welcome. He is in the child who knows nothing about Jesus or salvation, who does not have faith. He is in every human being, even the smallest and the defenseless.

The Eucharist, source of love for the life of the Church, is the school of charity and solidarity. Those who are nourished by the Bread of Christ cannot remain indifferent to those who do not have their daily bread. Today, we know it is an ever more serious problem.

May the feast of Corpus Christi increasingly inspire and nurture in each one of us the desire and commitment for a welcoming and supportive society. Let us pour these hopes into the heart of the Virgin Mary, Eucharistic woman. May she kindle in all the joy of participating in the Holy Mass, especially on Sundays, and the joyful courage to testify to the infinite love of Christ.

—Angelus Address, St. Peter's Square,
Solemnity of Corpus Christi, June 7, 2015

50. ABIDING IN JESUS
JOHN 15:1-8

Something Jesus often repeats, especially during the Last Supper, is "Abide in me" [John 15:4]. Do not tire of me; abide in me. And Christian life is precisely this: to abide in Jesus. This is Christian life: *to abide in Jesus*. And Jesus, in order to explain to us what he means by this, uses this beautiful figure of the vine: "I am the true vine, you the branches" (cf. 15:1). And every branch that is not joined to the vine ends up dying; it bears no fruit, and then is thrown away to feed the fire. Many are used for this, to feed the fire—they are very, very useful—but not in bearing fruit.

Rather, the branches that are united to the vine receive the lifeblood and thus develop, grow, and bear fruit. It's a simple, simple image. To abide in Jesus means to be united to him in order to receive life from him, love from him, the Holy Spirit from him. It's true, we are all sinners, but if we abide in Jesus, like the branches to the vine, the Lord comes. He prunes us a little so that we can bear more fruit. He always takes care of us. But if we detach from him, if we do not abide in the Lord, we are Christians in name only but not in life; we are Christians, but dead ones, because we bear no fruit, like branches broken away from the vine.

To abide in Jesus means to be willing to receive life from him, as well as pardon, even pruning, but to receive it from him. To abide in Jesus means to seek Jesus, to pray, prayer. To abide in Jesus means to approach the sacraments: the Eucharist,

Reconciliation. To abide in Jesus—and this is the most difficult thing—means to do what Jesus did, to have the same attitude as Jesus.

But when we "slur" someone else [speaking badly of others], for example, or when we gossip, we do not abide in Jesus. Jesus never did this. When we are liars, we do not abide in Jesus. He never did this. When we cheat others with the dirty deals that are available to everyone, we are dead branches; we do not abide in Jesus. To abide in Jesus is to do the things that he did: to do good, to help others, to pray to the Father, to care for the sick, to help the poor, to have the joy of the Holy Spirit.

A beautiful question for us Christians is this: do I abide in Jesus or am I far from Jesus? Am I united to the vine that gives me life, or am I a dead branch that is incapable of bearing fruit, giving witness? And there are other branches too, of which Jesus does not speak here, but he speaks about them elsewhere: those who make themselves look like disciples of Jesus, but they do the opposite of Jesus' disciples: these are hypocritical branches.

Perhaps they go to Mass every Sunday, perhaps their face looks like a holy card, all pious, but then they live like pagans. And Jesus calls them hypocrites in the Gospel. Jesus is good; he invites us to abide in him. He gives us the strength, and if we slide into sin—we are all sinners—he forgives us, because he is merciful. But what he wants are these two things: that we abide in him and that we are not hypocrites. And with this a Christian life moves forward.

And what does the Lord give us if we abide in him? We just heard it: "If you abide in me, and my words abide in you, ask whatever you will, and it shall be done for you" (John 15:7). The power of prayer: "Ask whatever you will"; that is, prayer is so powerful that Jesus does whatever we ask of him. However, if our prayer is weak—if it is not done sincerely in Jesus—prayer does not bear its fruit, because the branch is not united to the vine. But if the branch is united to the vine, that is, "If you abide in me, and my words abide in you, ask whatever you will, and it shall be done for you." And this is the almighty prayer.

Where does the omnipotence of this prayer come from? From abiding in Jesus, from being united to Jesus, like the branch to the vine. May the Lord grant us this grace.

—HOMILY, PASTORAL VISIT TO THE ROMAN PARISH
SANTA MARIA REGINA PACIS IN OSTIA,
MAY 3, 2015

51. FOLLOW THE PATH OF LOVE
JOHN 15:9-17

Today's Gospel—John, chapter 15—brings us back to the Last Supper, when we hear Jesus' new commandment. He says, "This is my commandment, that you love one another as I have loved you" (15:12). Thinking of his imminent sacrifice on the cross, he adds, "Greater love has no man than this, that a man lay down his life for his friends. You are my friends if you do what I command you" (15:13-14). These words, said at the Last Supper, summarize Jesus' full message. Actually, they summarize all that he did: Jesus gave his life for his friends. Friends who did not understand him—in fact, they abandoned, betrayed, and denied him at the crucial moment. This tells us that he loves us, even though we don't deserve his love. Jesus loves us in this way!

Thus, Jesus *shows us the path* to follow him: the path of love. His commandment is not a simple teaching which is always abstract or foreign to life. Christ's commandment is new because he realized it first; he gave his flesh, and thus the law of love is written upon the heart of man (cf. Jeremiah 31:33). And how is it written? It is written with the fire of the Holy Spirit. With this Spirit that Jesus gives us, we, too, can take this path!

It is a real path, a path that leads us to come out of ourselves and go toward others. Jesus showed us that the love of God *is realized in love for our neighbor.* Both go hand in hand. The pages of the Gospel are full of this love: adults and children, educated and uneducated, rich and poor, just and sinners: all were welcomed into the heart of Christ.

Therefore, this word of God calls us to love one another, even if we do not always understand each other and do not always get along . . . [It] is then that Christian love is seen. A love which manifests [itself] even if there are differences of opinion or character. Love is greater than these differences! This is the love that Jesus taught us. It is a new love because Jesus and his Spirit renewed it. It is a *redeeming love, free from selfishness*. A love which *gives our hearts joy*, as Jesus himself said: "These things I have spoken to you, that my joy may be in you, and that your joy may be full" (John 15:11).

It is precisely Christ's love that the Holy Spirit pours into our hearts to make everyday wonders in the Church and in the world. There are many *small and great actions* which obey the Lord's commandment: "Love one another as I have loved you" (John 15:12). Small everyday *actions, actions* of closeness to an elderly person, to a child, to a sick person, to a lonely person, those in difficulty, without a home, without work, an immigrant, a refugee . . . Thanks to the strength of the word of Christ, each one of us can make ourselves the brother or sister of those whom we encounter. Actions of closeness, actions which manifest the love that Christ taught us.

May our Most Holy Mother help us in this, so that in each of our daily lives, love of God and love of neighbor may be ever united.

—REGINA CAELI ADDRESS, ST. PETER'S SQUARE, MAY 10, 2015

52. WHERE IS MY HEART?
MATTHEW 26:14–27:66

This week begins with the festive procession with olive branches: the entire populace welcomes Jesus. The children and young people sing, praising Jesus.

But this week continues in the mystery of Jesus' death and his resurrection. We have just listened to the passion of our Lord. We might well ask ourselves just one question: who am I? Who am I, before my Lord? Who am I, before Jesus who enters Jerusalem amid the enthusiasm of the crowd? Am I ready to express my joy, to praise him? Or do I stand back? Who am I, before the suffering Jesus?

We have just heard many, many names. The group of leaders, some priests, the Pharisees, the teachers of the law, who had decided to kill Jesus. They were waiting for the chance to arrest him. Am I like one of them?

We have also heard another name: Judas. Thirty pieces of silver. Am I like Judas? We have heard other names too: the disciples who understand nothing, who fell asleep while the Lord was suffering. Has my life fallen asleep? Or am I like the disciples, who did not realize what it was to betray Jesus? Or like that other disciple, who wanted to settle everything with a sword? Am I like them?

Am I like Judas, who feigns love and then kisses the Master in order to hand him over, to betray him? Am I a traitor? Am I like those people in power who hastily summon a tribunal and seek false witnesses: am I like them? And when I do these things, if I do them, do I think that in this way I am saving the people?

Am I like Pilate? When I see that the situation is difficult, do I wash my hands and dodge my responsibility, allowing people to be condemned—or condemning them myself?

Am I like that crowd, which was not sure whether they were at a religious meeting, a trial, or a circus, and then chose Barabbas? For them it was all the same: it was more entertaining to humiliate Jesus.

Am I like the soldiers who strike the Lord, spit on him, insult him, who find entertainment in humiliating him?

Am I like the Cyrenean, who was returning from work, weary, yet was good enough to help the Lord carry his cross?

Am I like those who walked by the cross and mocked Jesus: "He was so courageous! Let him come down from the cross and then we will believe in him!" Mocking Jesus . . .

Am I like those fearless women, and like the mother of Jesus, who were there, and who suffered in silence?

Am I like Joseph, the hidden disciple, who lovingly carries the body of Jesus to give it burial?

Am I like the two Marys, who remained at the tomb, weeping and praying?

Am I like those leaders who went the next day to Pilate and said, "Look, this man said that he was going to rise again. We cannot let another fraud take place!" and who block life, who block the tomb, in order to maintain doctrine, lest life come forth?

Where is my heart? Which of these persons am I like? May this question remain with us throughout the entire week.

—HOMILY, ST. PETER'S SQUARE, CELEBRATION OF PALM SUNDAY,
APRIL 13, 2014

53. GOD CONQUERS IN FAILURE
MATTHEW 26:14-25

Today, midway through Holy Week, the liturgy presents us with a regrettable episode: the account of the betrayal of Judas, who goes to the leaders of the Sanhedrin to bargain for and deliver his master to them: "What will you give me if I deliver him to you?" (Matthew 26:15). At that moment, a price was set on Jesus. This tragic act marks the beginning of Christ's passion, a dolorous path which he chooses with absolute freedom. He himself says it clearly: "I lay down my life. . . . No one takes it from me, but I lay it down of my own accord. I have power to lay it down, and I have power to take it again" (John 10:17, 18). And thus by this betrayal, Jesus' journey of humiliation and despoliation begins. As though he were an article for sale: this one costs thirty pieces of silver. . . . Once he has taken the path of humiliation and self-abandonment, Jesus travels along it to the very end.

Jesus attains complete humiliation through "death on the cross." It was the worst form of death: that reserved for slaves and criminals. Jesus was considered a prophet, but he died like a criminal. As we contemplate Jesus in his passion, we see reflected the suffering of humanity, and we discover the divine answer to the mystery of evil, suffering, and death.

Many times we feel horror at the evil and suffering that surround us, and we ask ourselves, "Why does God allow it?" It deeply wounds us to see suffering and death, especially that of the innocent! When we see children suffer, it wounds our hearts:

it is the mystery of evil. And Jesus takes all of this evil, all of this suffering, upon himself. This week it would benefit all of us to look at the crucifix, to kiss the wounds of Jesus, to kiss them on the crucifix. He took upon himself all human suffering; he clothed himself in this suffering.

We expect God in his omnipotence to defeat injustice, evil, sin, and suffering with a triumphant divine victory. Yet God shows us a humble victory that, in human terms, appears to be failure. We can say that God conquers in failure! Indeed, the Son of God appears on the cross as a defeated man: he suffers, is betrayed, reviled, and finally dies. But Jesus allows evil to be unleashed on him, and he takes it upon himself in order to conquer it.

His passion is not an accident: his death—that death—was "written." Truly we cannot find many explanations. It is a puzzling mystery, the mystery of God's great humility: "For God so loved the world that he gave his only Son" (John 3:16). This week let us think deeply about the suffering of Jesus, and let us say to ourselves, "This is for my sake. Even if I had been the only person in the world, he would have done it. He did it for me." Let us kiss the crucifix and say, "For my sake, thank you, Jesus, for me."

When all seems lost, when no one remains, for they will strike "the shepherd, and the sheep of the flock will be scattered" (Matthew 26:31), it is then that God intervenes with the power of his resurrection. The resurrection of Jesus is not the happy ending to a nice story; it is not the "happy end" of a film; rather, it is God the Father's intervention there where human hope is shattered. At the moment when all seems to be lost, at the moment of suffering, when many people feel the need to get down from the cross, it is the moment closest to the resurrection. Night becomes darkest precisely before morning dawns, before the light dawns. In the darkest moment, God intervenes and raises.

Jesus, who chose to pass by this way, calls us to follow him on his own path of humiliation. When, at certain moments in life, we fail to find any way out of our difficulties, when we sink in the thickest darkness, it is the moment of our total humiliation and despoliation, the hour in which we experience that we are frail and are sinners. It is precisely then, at that moment, that we must not deny our failure but rather open ourselves trustingly to hope in God, as Jesus did.

Dear brothers and sisters, this week it will do us good to take the crucifix in hand and kiss it many, many times and say, "Thank you, Jesus, thank you, Lord." So be it.

—GENERAL AUDIENCE, ST. PETER'S SQUARE, WEDNESDAY IN
HOLY WEEK, APRIL 16, 2014

54. ENTER INTO THE MYSTERY
MARK 16:1-7

Tonight is a night of vigil. The Lord is not sleeping; the Watchman is watching over his people (cf. Psalm 121:4) to bring them out of slavery and to open before them the way to freedom.

The Lord is keeping watch, and, by the power of his love, he is bringing his people through the Red Sea. He is also bringing Jesus through the abyss of death and the netherworld.

This was a night of vigil for the disciples of Jesus, a night of sadness and fear. The men remained locked in the upper room. Yet the women went to the tomb at dawn on Sunday to anoint Jesus' body. Their hearts were overwhelmed and they were asking themselves, "How will we enter? Who will roll back the stone of the tomb? . . . " But here was the first sign of the great event: the large stone was *already* rolled back and the tomb was open!

"Entering the tomb, they saw a young man sitting on the right side, dressed in a white robe" (Mark 16:5). The women were the first to see this great sign, the empty tomb, and they were the first to enter.

"Entering the tomb." It is good for us, on this Vigil night, to reflect on the experience of the women, which also speaks to us. For that is why we are here: *to enter*, to *enter into the mystery* which God has accomplished with his *vigil of love.*

We cannot live Easter without entering into the mystery. It is not something intellectual, something we only know or read about. . . . It is more, much more!

"To enter into the mystery" means the ability to wonder, to contemplate; the ability to listen to the silence and to hear the tiny whisper amid great silence by which God speaks to us (cf. 1 Kings 19:12).

To enter into the mystery demands that we not be afraid of reality: that we not be locked into ourselves, that we not flee from what we fail to understand, that we not close our eyes to problems or deny them, that we not dismiss our questions.

To enter into the mystery means going beyond our own comfort zone, beyond the laziness and indifference which hold us back, and going out in search of truth, beauty, and love. It is seeking a deeper meaning, an answer, and not an easy one, to the questions which challenge our faith, our fidelity, and our very existence.

To enter into the mystery, we need humility, the lowliness to abase ourselves, to come down from the pedestal of our "I" which is so proud, of our presumption; the humility not to take ourselves so seriously, recognizing who we really are: creatures with strengths and weaknesses, sinners in need of forgiveness. To enter into the mystery, we need the lowliness that is powerlessness, the renunciation of our idols—in a word, we need to adore. Without adoration, we cannot enter into the mystery.

The women who were Jesus' disciples teach us all of this. They kept watch that night, together with Mary. And she, the Virgin Mother, helped them not to lose faith and hope. As a result, they did not remain prisoners of fear and sadness, but at the first light of dawn they went out carrying their ointments, their hearts anointed with love. They went forth and found the tomb open. And they went in. They had kept watch, they went forth, and they entered into the mystery. May we learn from them to keep watch with God and with Mary, our Mother, so that we, too, may enter into the mystery which leads from death to life.

—HOMILY, ST. PETER'S BASILICA, EASTER VIGIL, APRIL 4, 2015

55. RETURN TO GALILEE!
MATTHEW 28:1-10

The Gospel of the resurrection of Jesus Christ begins with the journey of the women to the tomb at dawn on the day after the Sabbath. They go to the tomb to honor the body of the Lord, but they find it open and empty. A mighty angel says to them, "Do not be afraid!" (Matthew 28:5) and orders them to go and tell the disciples, "He has been raised from the dead, and indeed he is going ahead of you to Galilee" (cf. 28:7). The women quickly depart, and on the way Jesus himself meets them and says, "Do not fear; go and tell my brothers to go to Galilee; there they will see me" (cf. 28:10). "Do not be afraid," "do not fear": these are words that encourage us to open our hearts to receive the message.

After the death of the Master, the disciples had scattered; their faith had been utterly shaken, everything seemed over, all their certainties had crumbled and their hopes had died. But now that message of the women, incredible as it was, came to them like a ray of light in the darkness. The news spread: Jesus is risen as he said. And then there was his command to go to *Galilee*; the women had heard it twice, first from the angel and then from Jesus himself: "Let them go to Galilee; there they will see me." "Do not fear" and "go to Galilee."

Galilee is *the place where they were first called, where every- thing began!* To return there, to return to the place where they were originally called. Jesus had walked along the shores of the lake as the fishermen were casting their nets. He had called them, and they left everything and followed him (cf. Matthew 4:18-22).

To return to Galilee means *to reread* everything on the basis of the cross and its victory, fearlessly: "Do not be afraid." To reread everything—Jesus' preaching, his miracles, the new community, the excitement and the defections, even the betrayal—to reread everything starting from the end, which is a new beginning, *from this supreme act of love.*

For each of us, too, there is a "Galilee" at the origin of our journey with Jesus. "To go to Galilee" means something beautiful; it means rediscovering our baptism as a living fountainhead, drawing new energy from the sources of our faith and our Christian experience. To return to Galilee means, above all, to return to that blazing light with which God's grace touched me at the start of the journey. From that flame I can light a fire for today and every day and bring heat and light to my brothers and sisters. That flame ignites a humble joy, a joy which sorrow and distress cannot dismay, a good, gentle joy.

In the life of every Christian, after baptism there is also another "Galilee," *a more existential "Galilee"*: the experience of a *personal encounter with Jesus Christ* who called me to follow him and to share in his mission. In this sense, returning to Galilee means treasuring in my heart the living memory of that call, when Jesus passed my way, gazed at me with mercy, and asked me to follow him. To return there means reviving the memory of that moment when his eyes met mine, the moment when he made me realize that he loved me.

Today, tonight, each of us can ask, *"What is my Galilee?"* I need to remind myself, to go back and remember. *"Where is my Galilee? Do I remember it? Have I forgotten it?"* Seek and you will find it! There the Lord is waiting for you. "Have I gone off on roads and paths which made me forget it? Lord, help me: tell me what my Galilee is, for you know that I want to return there to encounter you and to let myself be embraced by your mercy." Do not be afraid, do not fear, return to Galilee!

The Gospel is very clear: we need to go back there, to see Jesus risen and to become witnesses of his resurrection. This is not to go back in time; it is not a kind of nostalgia. It is returning to our first love, in order to *receive the fire* which Jesus has kindled in the world and to bring that fire to all people, to the very ends of the earth. Go back to Galilee, without fear!

"Galilee of the Gentiles" (Matthew 4:15; cf. Isaiah 9:1)! Horizon of the risen Lord, horizon of the Church; intense desire of encounter . . . Let us be on our way!

—Homily, St. Peter's Basilica, Easter Vigil, April 19, 2014

56. "WHY DO YOU SEEK THE LIVING AMONG THE DEAD?"

Luke 24:1-12

This week is the week of joy: we celebrate the resurrection of Jesus. It is a true and deep joy founded on the certainty that the risen Christ shall never die again; rather, he is alive and at work in the Church and in the world. This certainty has abided in the hearts of believers since that first Easter morning, when the women went to Jesus' tomb and the angels asked them, "Why do you seek the living among the dead?" (Luke 24:5).

"Why do you seek the living among the dead?" These words are like a milestone in history; but are also like a "stumbling block" if we do not open ourselves to the Good News, if we think that a dead Jesus is less bothersome than a Jesus who is alive! Yet how many times along our daily journey do we need to hear it said: "Why do you seek the living among the dead?" How often do we search for life among inert things, among things that cannot give life, among things that are here today and gone tomorrow, among the things that pass away . . . "Why do you seek the living among the dead?"

We need this when we shut ourselves in any form of selfishness or self-complacency; when we allow ourselves to be seduced by worldly powers and by the things of this world, forgetting God and neighbor; when we place our hope in worldly vanities, in money, in success. Then the word of God says to us, "Why do you seek the living among the dead? Why are you searching there? That thing cannot give you life! Yes, perhaps it will cheer you up for a moment, for a day, for a week, for a month . . . and then? Why do you seek the living among the dead?"

This phrase must enter into our hearts, and we need to repeat it. Shall we repeat it three times together? Shall we make the effort? Everyone: "Why do you seek the living among the dead?" *[Pope Francis repeats it with the crowd]*. Today when we return home, let us say it from the heart in silence, and let us ask ourselves this question: why in life do I seek the living among the dead? It will do us good.

It is not easy to be open to Jesus. Nor is it a given that we shall accept the life of the risen One and his presence among us. The Gospel shows us different reactions: that of the apostle Thomas, that of Mary Magdalene, and that of the two disciples of Emmaus; it does us good to compare ourselves with them. Thomas places a condition on belief; he asks to touch the evidence, the wounds. Mary Magdalene weeps; she sees him but she does not recognize him; she only realizes that it is Jesus when he calls her by name. The disciples of Emmaus, who are depressed and feeling defeated, attain an encounter with Jesus by allowing that mysterious wayfarer to accompany them. Each one on a different path! They were seeking the living among the dead, and it was the Lord himself who redirected their course. And what do I do? What route do I take to encounter the living Christ? He will always be close to us to correct our course if we have strayed.

"Why do you seek the living among the dead?" This question enables us to overcome the temptation to look back, to what was yesterday, and it spurs us on to the future. Jesus is not in the sepulcher; he is risen! He is the Living One, the One who always renews his body, which is the Church, and enables it to walk by drawing it toward him. "Yesterday" is the tomb of Jesus and the tomb of the Church, the tomb of truth and justice; "today" is the perennial resurrection to which the Holy Spirit impels us, bestowing on us full freedom.

Today this question is also addressed to us. You, why do seek the living among the dead, you who withdraw into yourself after a failure, and you who no longer have the strength to pray? Why do you seek the living among the dead, you who feel alone, abandoned by friends and perhaps also by God? Why do you seek the living among the dead, you who have lost hope, and you who feel imprisoned by your sins? Why do you seek the living among the dead, you who aspire to beauty, to spiritual perfection, to justice, and to peace?

We need to hear ourselves repeat and to remind one other of the angels' admonition! This admonition, "Why do you seek the living among the dead?" helps us leave behind our empty sadness and opens us to the horizons of joy and hope. That hope which rolls back the stones from tombs and encourages one to proclaim the Good News, capable of generating new life for others. Let us repeat the angels' phrase in order to keep it in our hearts and in our memory, and then let everyone respond in silence: "Why do you seek the living among the dead?" Let's repeat it! *[Pope Francis repeats it with the crowd]*. Behold, brothers and sisters, he is alive; he is with us! Do not go to the many tombs that today promise you something, beauty, and then give you nothing! He is alive! Let us not seek the living among the dead! Thank you.

—General Audience, St. Peter's Square, April 23, 2014

57. STRENGTHENED BY THE SPIRIT
JOHN 20:19-23

"As the Father has sent me, even so I send you. . . . Receive the Holy Spirit" (John 20:21, 22); this is what Jesus says to us. The gift of the Spirit on the evening of the resurrection took place once again on the day of Pentecost, intensified this time by extraordinary outward signs.

On the evening of Easter, Jesus appeared to the apostles and breathed on them his Spirit (cf. John 20:22); on the morning of Pentecost, the outpouring occurred in a resounding way, like a wind which shook the place the apostles were in, filling their minds and hearts. They received a new strength so great that they were able to proclaim Christ's resurrection in different languages: "They were all filled with the Holy Spirit and began to speak in other tongues, as the Spirit gave them utterance" (Acts 2:4). Together with them was Mary, the mother of Jesus, the first disciple, there too as mother of the nascent Church. With her peace, with her smile, with her maternity, she accompanied the joyful young bride, the Church of Jesus.

The word of God, especially in today's readings, tells us that the Spirit is at work in individuals and communities filled with himself; the Spirit makes them capable of *recipere Deum* [receiving God], *capax Dei* [with the capacity for God], as the holy Church Fathers say. And what does the Holy Spirit do with this new capability which he gives us? *He guides us into all the truth* (cf. John 16:13), *he renews the face of the earth* (cf. Psalm

104:30), and *he gives us his fruits* (cf. Galatians 5:22-23). He guides, he renews, and he makes fruitful.

In the Gospel, Jesus promises his disciples that, when he has returned to the Father, the Holy Spirit will come to guide them "into all the truth" (John 16:13). Indeed, he calls the Holy Spirit "the Spirit of truth," and explains to his disciples that the Spirit will bring them to understand ever more clearly what he, the Messiah, has said and done, especially in regard to his death and resurrection. To the apostles, who could not bear the scandal of their master's sufferings, the Spirit would give a new understanding of the truth and beauty of that saving event.

At first they were paralyzed with fear, shut in the upper room to avoid the aftermath of Good Friday. Now they would no longer be ashamed to be Christ's disciples; they would no longer tremble before the courts of men. Filled with the Holy Spirit, they would now understand "all the truth": that the death of Jesus was not his defeat, but rather the ultimate expression of God's love, a love that, in the resurrection, conquers death and exalts Jesus as the Living One, the Lord, the Redeemer of mankind, the Lord of history and of the world. This truth, to which the apostles were witnesses, became good news, to be proclaimed to all.

Then the Holy Spirit renews—guides and renews—*renews the earth*. The psalmist says, "You send forth your Spirit . . . and you renew the face of the earth" (cf. Psalm 104:30). The account of the birth of the Church in the Acts of the Apostles is significantly linked to this psalm, which is a great hymn of praise to God the Creator. The Holy Spirit whom Christ sent from the

Father, and the Creator Spirit who gives life to all things, are one and the same.

Respect for creation, then, is a requirement of our faith: the "garden" in which we live is not entrusted to us to be exploited but rather to be cultivated and tended with respect (cf. Genesis 2:15). Yet this is possible only if Adam—the man formed from the earth—allows himself in turn to be renewed by the Holy Spirit, only if he allows himself to be re-formed by the Father in the model of Christ, the new Adam.

In this way, renewed by the Spirit, we will indeed be able to experience the freedom of the sons and daughters, in harmony with all creation. In every creature we will be able to see reflected the glory of the Creator, as another psalm says: "How great is your name, O Lord our God, through all the earth!" (cf. Psalm 8:1, 9). He guides, he renews, and he gives; he gives fruits.

In the Letter to the Galatians, St. Paul wants to show the "fruits" manifested in the lives of those who walk in the way of the Spirit (cf. 5:22-23). On the one hand, he presents "the flesh," with its list of attendant vices: the works of selfish people closed to God. On the other hand, there are those who by faith allow the Spirit of God to break into their lives. In them, God's gifts blossom, summed up in nine joyful virtues which Paul calls "fruit of the Spirit." Hence his appeal, at the start and the end of the reading, as a program for life: "Walk by the Spirit" (5:16, 25).

The world needs men and women who are not closed in on themselves, but filled with the Holy Spirit. Closing oneself off from the Holy Spirit means not only a lack of freedom; it is a sin. There are many ways one can close oneself off to the Holy

Spirit: by selfishness for one's own gain; by rigid legalism—seen in the attitude of the doctors of the law to whom Jesus referred as "hypocrites"; by neglect of what Jesus taught; by living the Christian life not as service to others but in the pursuit of personal interests; and in so many other ways.

However, the world needs the courage, hope, faith, and perseverance of Christ's followers. The world needs the fruits, the gifts of the Holy Spirit, as St. Paul lists them: "love, joy, peace, patience, kindness, goodness, faithfulness, gentleness, self-control" (Galatians 5:22). The gift of the Holy Spirit has been bestowed upon the Church and upon each one of us so that we may live lives of genuine faith and active charity, that we may sow the seeds of reconciliation and peace.

Strengthened by the Spirit—who guides, who guides us into the truth, who renews us and the whole earth, and who gives us his fruits—strengthened in the Spirit and by these many gifts, may we be able to battle uncompromisingly against sin, to battle uncompromisingly against corruption, which continues to spread in the world day after day, by devoting ourselves with patient perseverance to the works of justice and peace.

—Homily, St. Peter's Basilica, Solemnity of Pentecost,
May 24, 2015

58. JESUS, THE FACE OF THE FATHER'S MERCY
JOHN 20:19-31

The Gospel according to John documents for us the two appearances of the risen Jesus to the apostles gathered in the upper room, where on the evening of Easter, Thomas was absent, and eight days later, he was present. The first time, the Lord showed them the wounds to his body, breathed on them, and said, "As the Father has sent me, even so I send you" (John 20:21). He imparts his same mission, through the power of the Holy Spirit.

But that night Thomas, who did not want to believe what the others witnessed, was not there. "Unless I see in his hands the print of the nails, and place my finger in the mark of the nails, and place my hand in his side," he said, "I will not believe" (John 20:25). Eight days later, Jesus returned to stand among them and turned immediately to Thomas, inviting him to touch the wounds in his hands and his side. He faced his incredulity so that, through the signs of the passion, he was able to reach the fullness of faith in the paschal mystery, namely, faith in the resurrection of Jesus.

Thomas was one who was not satisfied and seeks, intending to confirm himself, to have his own personal experience. After initial resistance and apprehension, in the end even he was able to believe; even though through effort, he came to believe. Jesus waited for him patiently and offered himself to the difficulties and uncertainty of the last to arrive. The Lord proclaimed "blessed" those who believe without seeing (John 20:29), the first of which is Mary, his mother.

He also met the needs of the doubting disciple: "Put your finger here, and see my hands" (John 20:27). In the redeeming contact with the wounds of the risen One, Thomas showed his own wounds, his own injuries, his own lacerations, his own humiliation; in the print of the nails he found the decisive proof that he was loved, that he was expected, that he was understood. He found himself before the Messiah filled with kindness, mercy, tenderness. This was the Lord he was searching for, he, in the hidden depths of his being, for he had always known [Jesus] was like this.

And how many of us are searching deep in our heart to meet Jesus, just as he is: kind, merciful, tender! For we know, deep down, that he is like this. Having rediscovered personal contact with Christ, who is amiable and mercifully patient, Thomas understood the profound significance of his resurrection and, intimately transformed, he declared his full and total faith in him, exclaiming, "My Lord and my God!" (John 20:28). Beautiful, Thomas' expression is beautiful!

He was able to "touch" the paschal mystery which fully demonstrated God's redeeming love (cf. Ephesians 2:4). All of us, too, are like Thomas: we are called to contemplate, in the wounds of the risen One, divine mercy, which overcomes all human limitations and shines on the darkness of evil and of sin. . . .

Jesus Christ is the face of the Father's mercy. Let us keep our gaze turned to him, who always seeks us, waits for us, forgives us; so merciful, he is not afraid of our wretchedness. In his wounds he heals us and forgives all of our sins. May the Virgin Mother help us to be merciful with others as Jesus is with us.

—Regina Caeli Address, St. Peter's Square, Divine Mercy Sunday, April 12, 2015

59. EMMAUS: A JOURNEY OF FAITH
LUKE 24:13-35

The Gospel from this Sunday, which is the Third Sunday of Easter, is that of the disciples of Emmaus. They were two of Jesus' disciples who, after his death and the Sabbath were past, leave Jerusalem and return, sad and dejected, to their village which was named Emmaus. Along the way the risen Jesus draws near to them, but they do not recognize him. Seeing them so sad, he first helps them to understand that the passion and death of the Messiah were foreseen in the plan of God and announced in the Sacred Scriptures: and thus he rekindled a fire of hope in their hearts.

At that point, the two disciples experienced an extraordinary attraction to the mysterious man, and they invited him to stay with them that evening. Jesus accepted and went into the house with them. When, at table, he blessed the bread and broke it, they recognized him, but he vanished out of their sight, leaving them full of wonder. After being enlightened by the word, they had recognized the risen Jesus in the breaking of the bread, a new sign of his presence. And immediately they felt the need to go back to Jerusalem to tell the other disciples about their experience, that they had met the living Jesus and recognized him in the act of the breaking of the bread.

The road to Emmaus thus becomes a symbol of our journey of faith: the Scriptures and the Eucharist are the indispensable elements for encountering the Lord. We, too, often go to Sunday Mass with our worries, difficulties, and disappointments. . . . Life sometimes wounds us, and we go away feeling sad, toward our "Emmaus," turning our backs on God's plan. We distance ourselves from God.

But the Liturgy of the Word welcomes us: Jesus explains the Scriptures to us and rekindles in our hearts the warmth of faith and hope, and in Communion he gives us strength. The word of God, the Eucharist. Read a passage of the Gospel every day. Remember it well: read a passage from the Gospel every day, and on Sundays go to Communion, to receive Jesus.

This is what happened to the disciples of Emmaus: they received the word, they shared the breaking of bread, and from feeling sad and defeated they became joyful. Dear brothers and sisters, the word of God and the Eucharist fill us with joy always. Remember it well! When you are sad, take up the word of God. When you are down, take up the word of God and go to Sunday Mass and receive Communion, to participate in the mystery of Jesus. The word of God, the Eucharist: they fill us with joy.

Through the intercession of Most Holy Mary, let us pray that every Christian, in reliving the experience of the disciples of Emmaus, especially at Sunday Mass, may rediscover the grace of the transforming encounter with the Lord, with the risen Lord, who is with us always. There is always a word of God that gives us guidance after we slip; and through our weariness and disappointments there is always a Bread that is broken that keeps us going on the journey.

—REGINA CAELI ADDRESS, ST. PETER'S SQUARE, MAY 4, 2014

60. WHO IS A WITNESS?
LUKE 24:35-48

In the Bible readings of today's liturgy, the word "witnesses" is mentioned twice. The first time, it is on the lips of Peter who, after the healing of the paralytic at the door of the Temple of Jerusalem, exclaims, "[You] killed the Author of life, whom God raised from the dead. To this we are witnesses" (Acts 3:15). The second time, it is on the lips of the risen Jesus. On the evening of Easter, he opens the minds of the disciples to the mystery of his death and resurrection, saying to them, "You are witnesses to these things" (cf. Luke 24:48).

The apostles, who saw the risen Christ with their own eyes, could not keep silent about their extraordinary experience. He had shown himself to them so that the truth of his resurrection would reach everyone by way of their witness. The Church has the duty to continue this mission over time. Every baptized person is called to bear witness, with their life and words, that Jesus is risen, that Jesus is alive and present among us. We are all called to testify that Jesus is alive.

We may ask ourselves: who is a witness? A witness is a person who has seen, who recalls, and [who] tells. *See, recall, and tell*: these are three verbs which describe the identity and mission. A witness is a person who has seen with an objective eye, has seen reality, but not with an indifferent eye; he *has seen* and has let himself become involved in the event. For this reason, one *recalls*, not only because she knows how to reconstruct the events exactly, but also because those facts spoke to her, and she grasped their profound meaning. Then a witness *tells*, not in a cold and detached way, but as one who has allowed himself to be called into question and from that day changed the way of life. A witness is someone who has changed his or her life.

The content of Christian witness is not a theory; it's not an ideology or a complex system of precepts and prohibitions or a moralist theory, but a message of salvation, a real event, rather, a Person: it is the risen Christ, the living and only Savior of all. He can be testified to by those who have personal experience of him, in prayer and in the Church, through a journey that has its foundation in baptism, its nourishment in the Eucharist, its seal in Confirmation, its continual conversion in penitence.

Thanks to this journey, ever guided by the word of God, every Christian can become a witness of the risen Jesus. And his or her witness is all the more credible, the more it shines through a life lived by the gospel: a joyful, courageous, gentle, peaceful, merciful life. Instead, if a Christian gives in to ease, vanity, selfishness, if he or she becomes deaf and blind to the question of "resurrection" of many brothers and sisters, how can he or she communicate the living Jesus; how can the Christian communicate the freeing power of the living Jesus and his infinite tenderness?

May Mary, our Mother, sustain us by her intercession, that we might become, with all our limitations but by the grace of faith, witnesses of the risen Lord, bringing the paschal gifts of joy and peace to the people we encounter.

—Regina Caeli Address, St. Peter's Square, April 19, 2015

the WORD among us®

The *Spirit* of Catholic Living

This book was published by The Word Among Us. Since 1981, The Word Among Us has been answering the call of the Second Vatican Council to help Catholic laypeople encounter Christ in the Scriptures.

The name of our company comes from the prologue to the Gospel of John and reflects the vision and purpose of all of our publications: to be an instrument of the Spirit, whose desire is to manifest Jesus' presence in and to the children of God. In this way, we hope to contribute to the Church's ongoing mission of proclaiming the gospel to the world so that all people would know the love and mercy of our Lord and grow ever more deeply in love with him.

Our monthly devotional magazine, *The Word Among Us*, features meditations on the daily and Sunday Mass readings, and currently reaches more than one million Catholics in North America and another half million Catholics in one hundred countries around the world. Our book division, The Word Among Us Press, publishes numerous books, Bible studies, and pamphlets that help Catholics grow in their faith.

To learn more about who we are and what we publish, log on to our website at www.wau.org. There you will find a variety of Catholic resources that will help you grow in your faith.

Embrace His Word, Listen to God . . .

www.wau.org